Steck Vaughn

Vocabulary Connections

Program Consultants

Dr. Barbara Coulter
Director, Department of Communication Arts
Detroit Public Schools

Dr. Catherine C. Hatala
Director, Reading/English Language Arts
School District of Philadelphia

Harcourt Achieve
Rigby • Steck-Vaughn

www.HarcourtAchieve.com
1.800.531.5015

ILLUSTRATIONS

Cover: Ed Lindlof
Content Area Logos: Skip Sorvino

Nancy Didion 36–39, 41, 115–116, 118; Eldon Doty 12–15, 17, 30–31, 33, 80–81, 83, 104–105, 107, 120–122, 124; Debbe Heller 61–63, 65, 108–111, 113; Bob Lange 52, 67; Jim McConnell 25–26, 28, 91–92, 94; Steven McIntosh 48–50; Ann Neumann 20, 22; Marcy Ramsey 42–44, 46, 66, 68, 70–74, 76; Freya Tanz 7–9, 11, 54–67, 59, 84–87, 89; Jean & Mou-sien Tseng 96–98, 100.

PHOTOGRAPHY

P. 5 © Bryan F. Peterson/Stock Market; p. 6 © The Bettmann Archive; pp. 18–19 © Joe Munroe/Photo Researchers, Inc.; pp. 23–24 © David Powers/Stock, Boston; p. 29 © Robert Reichert/Gamma-Liaison; p. 32 © Culver Pictures, Inc.; pp. 47, 60 © UPI/Bettmann Newsphotos; p. 53 © Simon Bruty/Allsport; p. 77 © Superstock; p. 78 © Verne Osdal/Black Star; p. 79 © AP/Wide World Photos; p. 90 © George Holton/Photo Researchers, Inc.; p. 95 © Paolo Koch/Photo Researchers, Inc.; pp. 102–103 © The Bettmann Archive; p. 114 © Pierre Berger/Photo Researchers, Inc.; p. 119 © Bill Strode/Black Star.

Additional photography by PhotoDisc/Getty Royalty Free.

ACKNOWLEDGMENTS

Doubleday: Excerpt from "The Continuing Search for . . . El Dorado, the City of Gold" by Faubion Bowers from *The People's Almanac* by David Wallechinsky and Irving Wallace. Copyright © 1975 by David Wallechinsky and Irving Wallace. Reprinted by permission of Doubleday, a division of Bantam, Doubleday, Dell Publishing Group, Inc.

HarperCollins Publishers: Adaptation from "The Canoe in the Rapids" from *The Talking Cat and Other Stories of French Canada* by Natalie Savage Carlson. Illustrated by Roger Duvoisin. COPYRIGHT © 1952 BY NATALIE SAVAGE CARLSON. Used by permission of HarperCollins Publishers. Adapted and abridged selection from *Olympic Champions: Why They Win* by Carli Laklan. TEXT COPYRIGHT © 1968 BY CARLI LAKLAN. Used by permission of HarperCollins Publishers.

Excerpt from MISTER STORMALONG by Anne Malcolmson and Dell McCormick. Copyright © 1952 by Mabel McCormick and Anne Burnett Malcolmson. Copyright © renewed 1980 by Anne Burnett Malcolmson Van Storch. Copyright © renewed 1980 by Joshua Tolford. Reprinted by permission of Houghton Mifflin Company. All rights reserved.

Macmillan Publishing Company: Pronunciation Key, reprinted with permission of the publisher from the *Macmillan School Dictionary 2.* Copyright © 1990 Macmillan Publishing Company, a division of Macmillan, Inc.

McGraw-Hill Inc.: From "Sequoyah" in *Word People* by Nancy Caldwell Sorel, copyright © 1970. Reprinted by permission of McGraw-Hill Inc.

ISBN 0-7398-9173-1

© 2004 Harcourt Achieve Inc.

3 4 5 6 7 8 073 11 10 09 08 07 06 05

TABLE OF CONTENTS

CONTENT AREA SYMBOLS ....

Literature   Social Studies   Science   Mathematics   Health   Fine Arts

RAMBLING RIVERS

Rivers can be as useful as they are beautiful. Not only do they provide transportation, they can also be a source of adventure!

In Lessons 1–4, you will read about rivers and their importance. Rivers are needed for many purposes. Think of some rivers you have seen or read about. How would you describe them? What activities could they be used for? Write your ideas on the lines below.

Words That Describe Rivers	River Activities
_____	_____
_____	_____
_____	_____
_____	_____
_____	_____

5

★ Read the story below. Think about the meanings of the **boldfaced** words. ★

River of Plenty

Imagine a river so long that it traces a path across the United States from coast to coast. Imagine, too, that this river continues for over a thousand miles. Then you'll have some idea of the length of Africa's river of plenty — the mighty Nile River. It begins near the **equator** and winds 4,145 miles northeast from the earth's middle. The Nile ends in Egypt, where it flows into the Mediterranean Sea. It is the longest river in the world.

The Nile, however, is not known only for its length. The Nile Valley, along with the **delta**, a three-sided stretch of lowland where the river ends, is one of the world's richest **agricultural** areas. For thousands of years, farmers have grown grains, vegetables, and cotton there.

The Nile River used to rise above its banks each year during the rainy season. The waters that flooded the land carried fine, rich soil called **silt**. When the rains stopped each September, the water on the flooded land **evaporated** into the air. What was left was moist, **fertile** farmland enriched with silt and ready for planting.

This cycle ended in 1968 when the Aswan High Dam was built. The dam created a **reservoir**, or lake, to hold the Nile's waters and stopped the yearly flooding. It also trapped the river's silt. Without this natural **resource**, the farmers of the Nile Valley were forced to use fertilizer to keep their soil rich. But the dam has also been helpful to farmers. It uses the river's power to generate electricity for farming, factory work, and other kinds of **industry**. It also provides water for land once too dry for farming.

People used to **worship** gods to pray for a good harvest. Now they turn to modern scientific methods. But just as in those ancient days, the Nile continues to be Africa's river of plenty.

★ Go back to the story. Underline the words or sentences that give you a clue to the meaning of each **boldfaced** word. ★

USING CONTEXT

Meanings for the vocabulary words are given below. Go back to the story and read each sentence that contains a vocabulary word. If you still cannot tell the meaning, look for clues in the sentences that come before and after the one with the vocabulary word. Write each word in front of its meaning.

industry	resource	agricultural	delta
worship	reservoir	evaporated	silt
equator	fertile		

1. _____ : three-sided stretch of lowland at the mouth of a river

2. _____ : having to do with farming

3. _____ : changed from a liquid into a gas or vapor, such as steam or fog

4. _____ : rich soil carried by water and deposited near riverbanks

5. _____ : able to produce crops easily; fruitful

6. _____ : business, trade, or production

7. _____ : a place where water collects and is stored, such as some lakes

8. _____ : pay honor and respect to something or someone considered sacred

9. _____ : a supply of something; something that meets a need

10. _____ : an imaginary line around the middle of the earth, midway between the North Pole and South Pole

CHALLENGE YOURSELF

Name two natural <u>resources</u>.

_____ _____

Name two things that have to do with an <u>agricultural</u> area.

_____ _____

7

WORD ORIGINS

Knowing the origin of a word can help you understand its meaning. Read each word origin. Then write each word from the box next to its origin.

fertile	reservoir	evaporate
resource	equator	

1. from Latin fertilis, fruitful _____

2. from Medieval Latin aequātor, thing that equalizes day and night _____

3. from Latin reservāre, to keep back or retain _____

4. from Latin resurgere, to rise up, lift _____

5. from Latin evapōratus, disappeared in vapor _____

CLOZE PARAGRAPH

Use the words in the box to complete the passage. Then reread the passage to be sure it makes sense.

resource	silt	industry	agricultural
evaporates	delta		

North of Cairo, the capital of Egypt, the Nile River creates an

area of land called a (1) _____. The soil here is
very rich and good for farming. It has been an important natural

(2) _____ for thousands of years. Every year,

floodwater from the Nile carries (3) _____, which
settles on the delta and enriches the land. When the water

(4) _____, it leaves the soil moist and ready for
growing. Because of the Nile River, the delta is not only an

(5) _____ area. Business and (6) _____
also benefit from the electricity created by the Nile's Aswan High Dam.

TANGLED-UP WORDS

A word is underlined in each sentence below. The word sounds similar to a word in the box. But its meaning makes it the wrong word for the sentence.

Read the paragraphs. Find the word in the box that should replace the underlined word. Write the vocabulary word on the line next to the number of the underlined word.

reservoir	industry	agricultural	delta
resource	worship	evaporates	silt
equator	fertile		

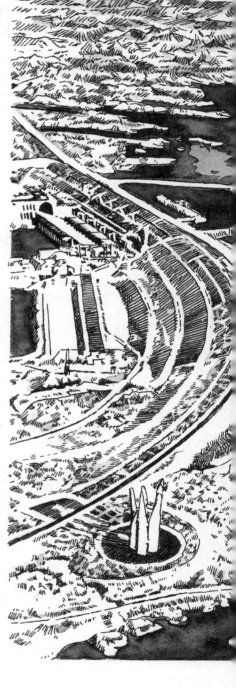

I learned that the Nile River begins near the (1) <u>equality</u> and ends in Egypt at the Mediterranean Sea. I hope someday to travel on part of this river to Egypt and see the rich (2) <u>agreeable</u> area of the (3) <u>belt</u>. I am told that if I pick up a handful of (4) <u>silk</u>, I will feel how moist this natural (5) <u>recorder</u> really is. I am also told that on the (6) <u>furious</u> farmland, I would see acres and acres of grains, vegetables, and cotton.

Another sight that I would visit is the (7) <u>register</u> formed by the Aswan High Dam. Some water from this lake (8) <u>erupts</u> over time. But the ever-flowing Nile River and the summer rains keep the lake filled.

When I travel to the cities of Cairo and Alexandria, I know I will see a lot of (9) <u>infantry</u>. Most factories are in these cities. The production of Egyptian cotton is a chief activity, and it keeps many, many workers very busy.

Of course, I haven't mentioned the most exciting of sights in Egypt — the pyramids. Who knows, maybe I'll ride a camel into the desert to see these amazing structures! For sure, it will be a trip back into time when people used to (10) <u>whisper</u> their gods and honor their kings.

1. _____   6. _____

2. _____   7. _____

3. _____   8. _____

4. _____   9. _____

5. _____   10. _____

GET WISE TO TESTS

Directions: Mark the space for the letter of the word that best completes the sentence.

Be sure to mark the answer space correctly. Do not mark the circle with an X or with a checkmark (✓). Instead, fill in the circle neatly and completely.

1. **Silt** is a kind of _____.
   - Ⓐ animal
   - Ⓑ soil
   - Ⓒ water
   - Ⓓ food

2. **Industry** has to do with _____.
   - Ⓕ teeth
   - Ⓖ air
   - Ⓗ writing plays
   - Ⓙ business

3. To **worship** is to _____ and respect someone.
   - Ⓐ ignore
   - Ⓑ honor
   - Ⓒ blame
   - Ⓓ forget

4. A **delta** is formed near a _____.
   - Ⓕ mountain
   - Ⓖ desert
   - Ⓗ river
   - Ⓙ sunset

5. The **equator** is an imaginary _____.
   - Ⓐ story
   - Ⓑ game
   - Ⓒ line
   - Ⓓ square

6. One kind of **agricultural** work is _____.
   - Ⓕ filing
   - Ⓖ running
   - Ⓗ writing
   - Ⓙ plowing

7. Land that is **fertile** is _____.
   - Ⓐ fruitful
   - Ⓑ rocky
   - Ⓒ hilly
   - Ⓓ poor

8. Water that has **evaporated** has turned into a _____.
   - Ⓕ solid
   - Ⓖ gas
   - Ⓗ liquid
   - Ⓙ stream

9. A **reservoir** is a _____.
   - Ⓐ soil
   - Ⓑ lake
   - Ⓒ song
   - Ⓓ crop

10. A **resource** is a _____ of something.
   - Ⓕ supply
   - Ⓖ picture
   - Ⓗ spoonful
   - Ⓙ report

Writing

The Nile River is very important to the people in Egypt and the surrounding areas. Is there a river, ocean, or lake near you that is important in your life?

Write a paragraph that tells about the body of water near you. Explain how it affects you in your life. Or if there is a river or ocean area that you would like to visit someday, tell about it. Explain why you are interested in it. Use some vocabulary words in your writing.

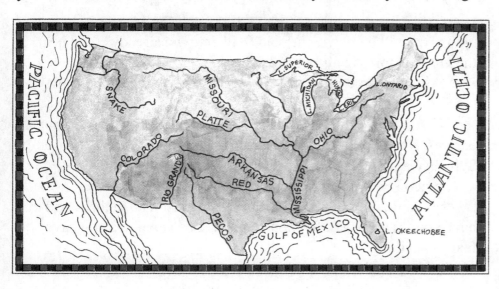

_____

_____

_____

_____

_____

_____

_____

_____

Turn to "My Personal Word List" on page 131. Write some words from the story or other words that you would like to know more about. Use a dictionary to find the meanings.

★ Read the story below. Think about the meanings of the **boldfaced** words. ★

The Canoe in the Rapids

Every spring, Canadian trappers Francois and Sylvain make a canoe trip to sell their catch to traders. This year, a surprise awaits them!

"A-ah, we will be rich men," said Sylvain, who already could hear the *tintin* of coins in his deep pockets.

"Yes," answered Francois, "if we get through the Devil's Jaws safely."

"That's true," said Sylvain, "but you are lucky to have me for a partner. Nowhere in all Canada is there such a skillful boatman as Sylvain Gagnon."

Francois rubbed his stubby chin.

"My faith," he exclaimed, "I am the luckiest man in the world to have you for a partner, Sylvain Gagnon. I don't believe you have fear of anything."

As if to test the truth of this, an angry growl came from behind the bushes. The bushes broke open and a big brown bear came through them. Francois dropped the gun and ran for his life. Already Sylvain Gagnon was far ahead of him, his fur coat making him look like a bear that ran too fast to shuffle from this paw to that paw.

Francois made for a big tree, but he didn't have time to climb it as the bear was almost on him. Francois lost no time in finding another tree to climb, for the tree they had been running around had been stripped of its bark as far up as a bear could reach.

Panting and dizzy himself, Francois settled into a crotch of the tree. Now where was that false friend, Sylvain Gagnon, who had left him to face the bear alone?

At last he jerkily lowered himself from the tree. Then great joy filled the heart of Francois Ecrette. Although the trees blackened the river, a faint moonlight glimmered through them. Its pale light fell upon a figure hunched in the bow of the canoe with the fur coat pulled up over its ears.

"Sylvain," cried Francois, "you are safe after all. Why didn't you come back to me?"

But Sylvain must have felt a deep shame, for he only put his head down between his arms and made a sad, apologetic sound.

"Believe me, my friend," said Francois, "I'm certainly glad you escaped, for we have a terrible ride ahead of us this night. Do you think we better try the **rapids** after all?"

But his companion **resolutely** straightened up and squared his shoulders in the fur coat. Francois felt the icy wind and the cold spray on his face as they plunged over the waterfall and bobbed in the **whirlpool** below. He fought the churning, **frothing** waters that he could hear more than see.

The **lurch** of the boat **wrenched** Francois Ecrette's back like a blow from a giant hammer. Around and around, up and down rocked the canoe, with Francois fiercely **wielding** his paddle. If it hadn't been for the soothing figure in front of him, he would have given up in fright.

Finally the canoe straightened out and leaped straight ahead.

"Ah, Sylvain," he yawned, "what a night we had in the rapids. If it hadn't been for you — a-tou-tou-tou-tou!"

For Francois Ecrette's partner in the canoe was not Sylvain Gagnon, the great boatman, but the big brown bear of the clearing!

Francois jumped up and gave a blood-curdling shriek. He dived into the river and furiously swam through the icy water. After what seemed a sinner's lifetime, he reached the frosty shore. He set out slowly. His boots **sloshed** and squashed through the **slush** of early spring.

It was late afternoon by the time he reached the trader's village. Everyone seemed surprised to see him alive. Then a familiar face appeared in the crowd.

"Francois, my good friend," cried Sylvain. "I got a ride back with a party of Indians. But how did you ever get the canoe through the rapids all by yourself?"

"Sylvain, my false friend," **retorted** the trapper, "I was not alone. The big brown bear who chased me in the clearing was with me."

Then Francois Ecrette shivered and shook in a way that had nothing to do with the cold spring afternoon or his damp clothing.

So all turned out well for Francois Ecrette in the end. But he never went on any more trapping trips with Sylvain Gagnon. You see, my friends, one who turns into a big brown bear when you need him most is not a true friend.

From The Talking Cat, and Other Stories of French Canada, by Natalie Savage Carlson

★ Go back to the story. Underline any words or sentences that give you clues to the meanings of the **boldfaced** words. ★

CONTEXT CLUES

In each sentence a word or phrase is underlined. Choose a word from the box to replace that word or phrase. Write the word on the line.

rapids	resolutely	frothing	lurch
wrenched	whirlpool	slush	retorted
wielding	sloshed		

1. Be careful of the <u>sudden movement</u> of a canoe if you are riding in one in rough water. _____

2. If you fall out of a canoe in rough water, the current may carry you through crashing, <u>bubbling</u> waters at the bottom of a falls. _____

3. The leader told how a man's back was <u>twisted sharply</u> after his canoe hit some large boulders. _____

4. The canoe finally made it to a calm part of the river where the waters gently <u>splashed</u> onto the bank. _____

5. The leader of the canoe adventure warned us that <u>strong, swift waters</u> can turn a canoe upside down. _____

6. A <u>swirling, circular current of water</u> can seem to swallow up anything. _____

7. I didn't know that in shallow water, people <u>using</u> paddles push off from the bottom of the river. _____

8. When a question about traveling down a river was posed to my friend, she <u>answered in a quick, sharp way</u>, "I want to travel in a canoe!" _____

9. The leaders asked her if she was prepared to face danger and uncomfortable weather conditions, including the <u>mud and melted snow</u> of early spring. _____

10. My friend stated <u>in a firm, determined way</u> that she was ready for any surprise the river had to offer her on a canoe journey.

_____

CLASSIFYING

Words can be grouped together to show what they have in common.
Write each word from the box in the group where it belongs.

rapids	wielding	whirlpool	slush
lurched	wrenched	sloshed	

Words related
to water: 1. _____   3. _____

2. _____

Words related
to action: 4. _____   6. _____

5. _____   7. _____

DICTIONARY SKILLS

Each numbered example has two parts. Answer the first part by
writing a word from the box. Answer the second part by circling
the correct choice. Use the **pronunciation key** in the Dictionary to
help you.

resolutely	frothing	wielding	retorted	wrenched

1. Write the correct spelling of wēld′ing.   _____

    It means   **a.** using   **b.** speaking

2. Write the correct spelling of rencht.   _____

    It means   **a.** pulled or twisted sharply   **b.** questioned

3. Write the correct spelling of frôth′ing.   _____

    It means   **a.** composing   **b.** bubbling

4. Write the correct spelling of
    rez′ə lüt′ lē.   _____

    It means   **a.** showing fear   **b.** showing strong determination

5. Write the correct spelling of ri tôrt′id.   _____

    It means   **a.** coughed loudly

                 b. answered in a quick, sharp way

GET WISE TO TESTS

Directions: Read each sentence. Pick the word that best completes the sentence. Mark the answer space for that word.

Before you choose an answer, try reading the sentence with each answer choice. This will help you choose an answer that makes sense.

Review

1. The spring rains filled the town _____.
   Ⓐ restaurant
   Ⓑ reservoir
   Ⓒ necessary
   Ⓓ important

2. The _____ workers are leaving the farms.
   Ⓕ everywhere
   Ⓖ advantage
   Ⓗ exciting
   Ⓙ agricultural

3. Many jobs in _____ offer higher pay.
   Ⓐ industry
   Ⓑ healthy
   Ⓒ invasion
   Ⓓ rivers

4. The jungles near the _____ are hot and steamy.
   Ⓕ inventor
   Ⓖ equator
   Ⓗ afterward
   Ⓙ enemy

1. He _____ answered the question with a loud yes.
   Ⓐ swam
   Ⓑ whirlpool
   Ⓒ although
   Ⓓ resolutely

2. The canoe bounced over the rough river _____.
   Ⓕ wielding
   Ⓖ rapids
   Ⓗ seems
   Ⓙ rather

3. A small spring flower poked through the melting _____.
   Ⓐ slush
   Ⓑ lurch
   Ⓒ necessary
   Ⓓ often

4. As we rode the waves, the _____ of the boat made me seasick.
   Ⓕ retorted
   Ⓖ lunch
   Ⓗ arranges
   Ⓙ lurch

5. A _____ pulled the fish down to the river bottom.
   Ⓐ beyond
   Ⓑ whirlpool
   Ⓒ cloud
   Ⓓ wrenched

6. The water was _____ at the bottom of the falls.
   Ⓕ frothing
   Ⓖ retorted
   Ⓗ designer
   Ⓙ slips

7. "Of course I can help you," the rescue worker _____.
   Ⓐ themselves
   Ⓑ sloshed
   Ⓒ resolutely
   Ⓓ retorted

8. The woman, _____ a large sign, spoke excitedly to the news reporter.
   Ⓕ frothing
   Ⓖ wielding
   Ⓗ grief
   Ⓙ nevertheless

9. The athlete _____ her arm doing a flip.
   Ⓐ generous
   Ⓑ retorted
   Ⓒ primitive
   Ⓓ wrenched

10. The children wearing boots _____ through the puddle.
   Ⓕ whirlpool
   Ⓖ resolutely
   Ⓗ sloshed
   Ⓙ playfulness

Writing

At the end of the tale, the narrator says, "One who turns into a big brown bear when you need him most is not a true friend." What does the author mean? Do you agree? What qualities do you think are most important in a friend?

Write a paragraph expressing your thoughts and feelings. You might wish to include some examples of how someone you know is a friend to you, or how you are a friend to someone else. Use some vocabulary words in your writing.

Turn to "My Personal Word List" on page 131. Write some words from the story or other words that you would like to know more about. Use a dictionary to find the meanings.

★ Read the story below. Think about the meanings of the **boldfaced** words. ★

Time and a River

Go back in time more than a billion years. There were no people living on Earth. Our planet was nothing like it is today. But processes were in motion to create today's amazing natural wonders. One of those wonders — the Grand Canyon — was formed by time and a river.

Earthquakes and volcanoes shook the earth a billion years ago. Layers of rock deep in the earth's **interior** were pushed upward, breaking through the surface. After many centuries, these rock layers were covered by seas, now long gone. As time passed, these seas **receded**. As they pulled back, they caused the rock to **protrude** above the earth's surface. The enormous flat rock that stuck out was 4,000 feet thick. Formed nearly ten million years ago, this huge **plateau** sat like a giant stone layer cake in what is now Arizona. **Erosion** caused by wind, rain, and sand began to carve ragged shapes in the rock.

A river was also at work, eating away at the stone. Today that river is known as the Colorado River. Like the wind and water, the river worked slowly but steadily. At the rate of one inch per 100 years, it carved a path through the rock. It was this river that created the Grand Canyon in the huge plateau.

Scientists who study the Grand Canyon have helped to piece together what we know about how it was formed. Small **clefts** in the rock offer clues. In these openings, scientists have found fossils of long-dead sharks and shellfish **embedded** in the rock. These buried remains tell us that seawater once covered the rock.

In 1869, John Wesley Powell followed the Colorado River into the canyon. Far from finding it **desolate**, he saw animals and a tribe of Native Americans living in the canyon. Powell stood on the **brink** of a cliff, looked down from the edge into the **chasm**, and called it "grand." From that time on, we have known this natural wonder as the Grand Canyon.

★ Go back to the story. Underline the words or sentences that give you a clue to the meaning of each **boldfaced** word. ★

CONTEXT CLUES

Read each sentence. Look for clues to help you complete each sentence with a word from the box. Write the word on the line.

erosion	chasm	embedded	clefts
receded	plateau	desolate	brink
interior	protrude		

1. To stand at the _____, or edge, of a cliff and look down into the Grand Canyon is to look back into more than a billion years of history.

2. The Grand Canyon had its origins in layers of rock deep in the earth's _____, which were pushed upward by earthquakes and volcanoes.

3. These rock layers were covered by ancient seas until the waters _____, or pulled back.

4. This caused the massive rock to _____ above the earth's surface in an area that is now part of the state of Arizona.

5. A huge _____ had been formed that looked like a giant stone layer cake.

6. The process of _____, the wearing away of rock by the wind, water, and sand, cut shapes and paths in the plateau.

7. Clues in the form of fossils of long-dead sharks and shellfish _____ in the rock have given scientists information about the canyon's history.

8. Scientists looked into small _____, or cracks, where these fossils were found enclosed in the ten-million-year-old rock.

9. It was John Wesley Powell who looked down into the _____ and felt that the only word for it was "grand."

10. With all its visitors, the Grand Canyon will never be a _____ place.

WORD ORIGINS

Remember that knowing the origin of a word can help you understand its meaning. Read each word origin. Then write each word from the box next to its origin.

cleft	plateau	desolate	recede
chasm	erosion	protrude	

1. from French platel, flat object _____

2. from Latin ērōsiōn, gnawing away _____

3. from Old English clyft, split _____

4. from Latin recēdere, go; fall back _____

5. from Latin dēsōlāre, to make lonely _____

6. from Latin prō + trūdere, to thrust _____

7. from Greek cha + (a)sma, to gape _____

ANALOGIES

An **analogy** compares two pairs of words. The relationship between the first pair of words is the same as the relationship between the second pair of words. For example, Finger is to hand as toe is to foot. Use the words in the box to complete the following analogies.

brink	plateau	interior
recede	chasm	

1. Middle is to center as edge is to _____.

2. Under is to below as inside is to _____.

3. Small is to cleft as huge is to _____.

4. Rounded is to hill as flat is to _____.

5. Progress is to advance as retreat is to _____.

GET WISE TO TESTS

Directions: Read the phrase. Look for the word or words that have the same or almost the same meaning as the boldfaced word. Mark the answer space for your choice.

 Some tests have letters in the answer circles. Fill in the circle next to your answer, being sure to cover the letter, too.

Review

1. wide **plateau**
   - Ⓐ flat rock
   - Ⓑ slope
   - Ⓒ peak
   - Ⓓ clefts

2. soil **erosion**
   - Ⓕ planting
   - Ⓖ an adding to
   - Ⓗ a wearing away
   - Ⓙ growing

3. a deep **chasm**
   - Ⓐ river
   - Ⓑ opening
   - Ⓒ voice
   - Ⓓ plateau

4. slowly **receded**
   - Ⓕ advanced
   - Ⓖ raised
   - Ⓗ pulled back
   - Ⓙ poured in

5. tiny **clefts**
   - Ⓐ plateaus
   - Ⓑ bridges
   - Ⓒ fossils
   - Ⓓ cracks

6. the **brink** of
   - Ⓕ bottom
   - Ⓖ edge
   - Ⓗ request
   - Ⓙ interior

7. lovely **interior**
   - Ⓐ outside
   - Ⓑ inside
   - Ⓒ clefts
   - Ⓓ music

8. cause to **protrude**
   - Ⓕ miss out
   - Ⓖ shut out
   - Ⓗ fall out
   - Ⓙ stick out

9. **desolate** place
   - Ⓐ lonely
   - Ⓑ delicate
   - Ⓒ busy
   - Ⓓ distant

10. **embedded** in
   - Ⓕ slept
   - Ⓖ enclosed
   - Ⓗ floated
   - Ⓙ receded

1. **fertile** land
   - Ⓐ useless
   - Ⓑ dry
   - Ⓒ fruitful
   - Ⓓ foreign

2. rich **silt**
   - Ⓕ food
   - Ⓖ soil
   - Ⓗ reservoir
   - Ⓙ stone

3. natural **resource**
   - Ⓐ record
   - Ⓑ equator
   - Ⓒ support
   - Ⓓ supply

4. **worship** gods
   - Ⓕ pay honor to
   - Ⓖ walk away from
   - Ⓗ sing about
   - Ⓙ work with

5. big **industry**
   - Ⓐ story
   - Ⓑ business
   - Ⓒ lake
   - Ⓓ silt

Many people have seen or are planning to see the Grand Canyon. Is there a place in the United States that you have always wanted to visit?

Write a paragraph telling about a place you hope to visit someday. These signs may give you some ideas. Describe some things that you find exciting or interesting about them. Use some vocabulary words in your writing.

_____

_____

_____

_____

_____

_____

_____

_____

_____

_____

_____

_____

_____

_____

_____

Turn to "My Personal Word List" on page 131. Write some words from the story or other words that you would like to know more about. Use a dictionary to find the meanings.

★ Read the story below. Think about the meanings of the **boldfaced** words. ★

Down a Wild River

A spray of water hits you in the face as your raft swirls through the foaming **tempest**. Someone shouts, "There's a rock ahead!" Quickly, you and your crewmates turn the raft to avoid striking the rock and perhaps tipping over. You are white-water rafting. And it's a thrill!

"White water" is the name given to river rapids. White water forms where a riverbed narrows and drops sharply. There the water **cascades** and tumbles down and around rocks. Rafters must know how to move their large rubber boats safely over these rushing waters.

Safety is very important in white-water rafting. Before setting off, everyone puts on a life jacket. Each raft, which may carry between 10 and 20 people, has a guide aboard. The guide is a person who knows the river and the rapids. Before **departure**, the guide gives the crew members important lessons. They learn how to **pivot** the raft to direct it around rocks, hidden tree trunks, and other dangers. They also learn what to do if a person is thrown out **midstream**.

Falling out of a raft in the middle of a river can be a frightening **ordeal**. Hitting the ice-cold water makes you shiver and gasp for breath. But even scarier is knowing that you will have to fight the rushing waters alone for a while. Not until the raft reaches calmer waters can a **lifeline** be thrown out. Only then can you be pulled back aboard.

Often a whole raft will turn over. Then the rafters know to head for the **shoreline**. There, on the bank of the river, they check to make sure that everyone is safe.

A run down a river can take as little as three or four hours. But people who enjoy white-water rafting often take **backpacking** trips. Hiking by day and camping by night, these nature lovers explore **remote** areas that are still wild and untouched by civilization.

★ Go back to the story. Underline the words or sentences that give you a clue to the meaning of each **boldfaced** word. ★

CONTEXT CLUES

In each sentence a word or phrase is underlined. Choose a word from the box to replace that word or phrase. Write the word on the line.

departure	shoreline	backpacking	remote
cascades	midstream	lifeline	pivot
tempest	ordeal		

1. Rafting is usually fun, but for beginning rafters it could be an <u>awfully harsh experience</u>. _____

2. Before <u>leaving</u>, you must be given some instructions about rafting. _____

3. You will learn how to <u>turn</u> the raft to direct it around rocks and other hidden dangers. _____

4. You will also learn how to use a <u>lifesaving rope</u>.

   _____

5. Another important instruction has to do with difficult situations in the <u>middle of the river</u>. _____

6. If a raft overturns, you must get to the <u>land on either side of the river</u> as quickly as you can. _____

7. If safety rules are followed, riding the <u>storm of swirling, foaming water</u> can be thrilling. _____

8. Today's nylon and rubber rafts are sturdy enough to take the rushing water that <u>tumbles and falls</u> down rocks.

   _____

9. When you are finished rafting, you can go <u>hiking while carrying supplies in a pack on your back</u>. _____

10. If you hike and raft, you can explore <u>distant, out-of-the-way</u> areas along a river. _____

WORD GROUPS

Read each pair of words. Think about how they are alike. Write the word from the box that best completes each group.

departure	lifeline	backpacking
ordeal	remote	shoreline

1. hiking, camping, _____

2. beach, riverbank, _____

3. leaving, going, _____

4. lifeguard, lifeboat, _____

5. distant, faraway, _____

6. test, trial, _____

DICTIONARY SKILLS

Write the words in alphabetical order, one word on each line. Then turn to the Dictionary, beginning on page 133. Find each word in the Dictionary and write its meaning below.

ordeal	pivot	cascades	backpacking
remote	tempest	midstream	departure

1. _____

2. _____

3. _____

4. _____

5. _____

6. _____

7. _____

8. _____

HIDDEN MESSAGE PUZZLE

Write a word from the box next to each clue. To find the message, copy the numbered letters above the matching numbered spaces at the bottom of the page. Then you will know how you might feel after going white-water rafting.

remote	midstream	cascades	backpacking
pivot	departure	tempest	lifeline
ordeal	shoreline		

1. leaving — — — — — — —
                    1

2. water's edge — — — — — — — —
                        8

3. falls, tumbles — — — — — — — —
                              3

4. far off — — — — — —
         4

5. a rope thrown
   to a drowning
   person — — — — — — — —
                    5

6. turn — — — — —
            6

7. in the middle
   of the river — — — — — — — — —

8. hiking while
   carrying
   supplies — — — — — — — — — — —
                                      7

9. a storm of
   swirling,
   foaming water — — — — — — —
              2

10. a severe
    experience — — — — — —
              9

ANSWER: W — — — — — — — — — — !
            1 2 3 4 5 6 7 7 8 9

GET WISE TO TESTS

Directions: Choose the word or words that best take the place of the boldfaced word.

Tip This test will show how well you understand the meaning of the words. Think about the meaning of the boldfaced word before you choose your answer.

1. Lisa was ready for the **ordeal**. She knew about the dangerous rapids.
   Ⓐ restaurant
   Ⓑ tournament
   Ⓒ harsh experience
   Ⓓ life

2. We rafted through the **tempest**. What a wet ride!
   Ⓕ shoreline
   Ⓖ snowstorm
   Ⓗ time period
   Ⓙ swirling water

3. Keep a **lifeline** on the boat. Be prepared for accidents.
   Ⓐ map
   Ⓑ emergency kit
   Ⓒ rope
   Ⓓ tempest

4. Look at the **shoreline**. We are not far from land.
   Ⓕ lake
   Ⓖ water's edge
   Ⓗ mountain
   Ⓙ lifeline

5. We went **backpacking** in the woods. We walked for miles!
   Ⓐ swimming
   Ⓑ fishing
   Ⓒ digging
   Ⓓ hiking

6. I fell out of the boat **midstream**. I swam to shore.
   Ⓕ in the middle
   Ⓖ at the end
   Ⓗ in the back
   Ⓙ at the start

7. The people live in a **remote** village. It is a wild area.
   Ⓐ ancient
   Ⓑ nearby
   Ⓒ large
   Ⓓ distant

8. The river **cascades**. It becomes a waterfall.
   Ⓕ rises up
   Ⓖ stops flowing
   Ⓗ tumbles down
   Ⓙ flows

9. We can **pivot** the boat. We can direct it easily.
   Ⓐ lift
   Ⓑ stand in
   Ⓒ carry
   Ⓓ turn

10. I had an early **departure**. I packed and went quickly.
    Ⓕ visit
    Ⓖ stopping
    Ⓗ leaving
    Ⓙ tempest

Review

1. The **interior** of the house was changed. The rooms were large.
   Ⓐ inside
   Ⓑ outside
   Ⓒ front
   Ⓓ back

2. The tide **receded**. Many seashells were left on the beach.
   Ⓕ surged ahead
   Ⓖ lifted
   Ⓗ pulled back
   Ⓙ overflowed

3. She is on the **brink** of the ice. Open water is beyond.
   Ⓐ cracks
   Ⓑ edge
   Ⓒ level
   Ⓓ ridges

4. There are **clefts** in the stone. Small animals live in them.
   Ⓕ small trees
   Ⓖ big caves
   Ⓗ small openings
   Ⓙ layers

Writing

Both rafting and hiking are fun sports for many people. Which sport would you prefer? Would it be riding the foaming, swirling waters or walking through the peaceful, cool woods?

Write a paragraph that compares and contrasts the two sports. Explain ways they are alike and different. Also tell which sport you would prefer and why. Use some vocabulary words in your writing.

_____

_____

_____

_____

_____

_____

_____

_____

_____

_____

_____

_____

_____

_____

_____

_____

_____

_____

Turn to "My Personal Word List" on page 131. Write some words from the story or other words that you would like to know more about. Use a dictionary to find the meanings.

★ To review the words in Lessons 1–4, turn to page 125. ★

EXTRAORDINARY INVENTIONS

Once radio and television were new inventions. Today they are part of our daily lives. Now the computer, a more recent invention, is becoming increasingly common.

In Lessons 5–8, you will read about some famous inventors and their inventions. Without the ideas of these creative people, our lives would be very different today. Think about some important inventions. How does each make your life easier? Write your ideas on the lines below.

Important Inventions	**How They Help People**

29

★ Read the story below. Think about the meanings of the **boldfaced** words. ★

A Man of Vision

Almost everyone believes that Ben Franklin flew a kite in a thunderstorm. According to the story, lightning struck his kite and made sparks fly from a key that he had tied to the string. Also according to the story, people thought he was crazy.

It is not always easy for inventors to get people to **comprehend** their new ideas. This must have been true for Ben Franklin. He was full of many **progressive** ideas.

Supposedly Franklin flew a kite to **illustrate** that lightning is electricity. Even though he did not do the experiment with the kite, he did learn that lightning is electricity. And he used what he had learned to invent the lightning rod. This simple metal rod was attached to a roof. His **prediction** that lightning would travel down the rod to the ground and save a building from catching fire was correct. Everyone could **benefit** from his idea.

Franklin had other ideas that helped people. He made **bifocal** glasses that had two kinds of lenses to enable people to see better. He made a stove that saved fuel and heated a room better than others. But he would never **patent** his inventions to stop others from stealing his ideas.

We benefit today from Franklin's wish to help others. In Philadelphia, he **established** the police and fire departments. He also started a public library, university, and hospital. Next time you check the mailbox, remember that Franklin was the **founder** of the U.S. Postal Service.

Perhaps Benjamin Franklin's most **significant** contribution was helping create the United States. He signed both the Declaration of Independence and the Constitution.

Ben Franklin was truly a man of vision, with an eye to the future. He made many contributions, not only as an inventor, but also as a public servant and statesman.

★ Go back to the story. Underline the words or sentences that give you a clue to the meaning of each **boldfaced** word. ★

CONTEXT CLUES

Read each sentence. Look for clues to help you complete each
sentence with a word from the box. Write the word on the line.

prediction	comprehend	bifocal	benefit
illustrate	significant	founder	patent
established	progressive		

1. When people think about the number and variety of Benjamin

   Franklin's contributions, they can't quite _____
   how he did it all.

2. He didn't care about protecting the rights to his ideas in order to
   prevent them from being stolen, so he didn't

   _____ his inventions.

3. His _____, or forward-thinking, ideas
   continue to help people today in areas of government, science,
   and public services.

4. The founding of a university, the starting of a public library, and
   the forming of the police and fire departments all help to

   _____, or show, Franklin's desire to help
   others.

5. Franklin's invention of _____ glasses, in
   which two lenses were put together to help people see better,
   was another great idea.

6. But perhaps Franklin's most _____
   contribution had to do with the creation of our nation.

7. He was a signer of the Declaration of Independence, which

   _____ the colonies' freedom from England.

8. The country continued to _____, or gain, from
   Franklin's wisdom and help in shaping the Constitution in 1787.

9. Franklin's _____ that the new nation would
   survive all its problems has certainly come true.

10. Along with George Washington, Benjamin Franklin can be

    considered a _____ of the United States.

MULTIPLE MEANINGS

The words in the box have more than one meaning. Look for clues in each sentence to tell which meaning is being used. Write the letter of the meaning next to the correct sentence.

established
a. set up on a lasting basis
b. showed beyond a doubt; proved

progressive
a. forward thinking
b. developing or advancing in seriousness

benefit
a. receive good or gain from
b. a performance to raise money for a cause

illustrate
a. make clear or explain by giving examples
b. show something in a picture, drawing, or diagram

_____ 1. The lawyer established that the man was guilty.

_____ 2. Franklin established the police and fire departments.

_____ 3. Franklin had more progressive ideas than most other people.

_____ 4. It is a progressive disease, so it won't be cured quickly.

_____ 5. There will be a benefit for college scholarships.

_____ 6. We can all benefit from this man's ideas.

_____ 7. Franklin's inventions illustrate his concerns for other people.

_____ 8. We can illustrate the bifocal lenses on this paper.

SYNONYMS

Synonyms are words that have the same or almost the same meaning. Circle the words in each row that are synonyms.

1. uncomfortable   understand   comprehend

2. illustrate   explain   injure

3. prediction   protection   forecast

4. significant   silly   important

5. founder   catcher   creator

Tangled-up Words

A word is underlined in each sentence below. The word sounds similar to a word in the box. But its meaning makes it the wrong word for the sentence.

Read the paragraphs. Find the word in the box that should replace the underlined word. Write the vocabulary word on the line next to the number of the underlined word.

significant	prediction	bifocal	benefit
comprehended	illustrate	founder	patent
established	progressive		

If I had lived in the days of Ben Franklin, I most likely would not have (1) complicated what he was trying to do with a metal rod attached to the top of a barn roof. I would have thought, "This man is crazy. Anyone can (2) irritate that lightning is fire." But later, when I learned what he had discovered, I would have understood that his invention was a very (3) magnificent one. His (4) preparation that lightning would travel down the rod proved to be correct. His invention of the lightning rod could save a barn or other building from catching fire. People certainly did (5) misfit from it!

Franklin invented or (6) distinguished so many things that would have kept my head spinning, along with everyone else's. I would have marveled at his invention of (7) bicycle glasses. I would have been thankful that he started a public library, university, and hospital. I would have been grateful that he was the (8) flounder of the U.S. Postal Service.

Although the time of Ben Franklin must have been very exciting, I'm glad I live today so that I can enjoy the results of all Franklin's work. I can look back and see how (9) protective his ideas were for his time. I can say that I'll never quite understand why he didn't (10) satin his inventions. But I can also say that I'm glad he was such a great inventor, public servant, and statesman.

1. _____

2. _____

3. _____

4. _____

5. _____

6. _____

7. _____

8. _____

9. _____

10. _____

GET WISE TO TESTS

Directions: Read each sentence. Pick the word that best completes the sentence. Mark the answer space for that word.

Some tests put letters before the answer choices. Be sure to find the letter of the answer you think is correct, and then fill in the circle beside it.

Review

1. We can see the _____ from the boat.
   Ⓐ walked
   Ⓑ shoreline
   Ⓒ remote
   Ⓓ watery

2. The storm has turned the river into a foaming _____.
   Ⓕ tempest
   Ⓖ temperature
   Ⓗ rough
   Ⓙ waving

3. They live in a _____ area, far from the nearest town.
   Ⓐ beauty
   Ⓑ vastly
   Ⓒ remote
   Ⓓ removing

4. Use this rope as a _____ in case anyone falls out of the boat.
   Ⓕ buoyed
   Ⓖ safely
   Ⓗ shoreline
   Ⓙ lifeline

1. The teacher showed a picture to _____ his point.
   Ⓐ patent
   Ⓑ illustrate
   Ⓒ confusion
   Ⓓ fortunately

2. It is wise to _____ your inventions.
   Ⓕ creative
   Ⓖ patent
   Ⓗ vivid
   Ⓙ founder

3. We did not _____ the size of the problem.
   Ⓐ comprehend
   Ⓑ established
   Ⓒ teacher
   Ⓓ realistic

4. The man saw more clearly through his _____ glasses.
   Ⓕ benefit
   Ⓖ broken
   Ⓗ playfully
   Ⓙ bifocal

5. Early settlers _____ our town in 1750.
   Ⓐ founder
   Ⓑ drive
   Ⓒ often
   Ⓓ established

6. Everyone can _____ from Ben Franklin's inventions.
   Ⓕ founder
   Ⓖ although
   Ⓗ benefit
   Ⓙ sicken

7. Our new mayor has fresh and _____ ideas.
   Ⓐ progressive
   Ⓑ stale
   Ⓒ prediction
   Ⓓ worshipped

8. The _____ of our school spoke to the graduates.
   Ⓕ progressive
   Ⓖ founder
   Ⓗ terribly
   Ⓙ moving

9. The scientist's _____ later proved correct.
   Ⓐ comprehend
   Ⓑ vote
   Ⓒ prediction
   Ⓓ significant

10. The telephone is a _____ invention.
    Ⓕ prediction
    Ⓖ significant
    Ⓗ overly
    Ⓙ bifocal

Writing

Inventing something can be very exciting and rewarding. What would you like to invent and patent? Would it be something to ride in, a new kind of telephone, or perhaps a new machine?

Write a paragraph telling about your invention. Give it a name, tell how it works, and explain its uses. Draw a picture of it below. Use some vocabulary words in your writing.

Turn to "My Personal Word List" on page 131. Write some words from the story or other words that you would like to know more about. Use a dictionary to find the meanings.

★ Read the story below. Think about the meanings of the **boldfaced** words. ★

Sequoyah and the Talking Leaf

While living in the Cherokee territory of Tennessee, young Sequoyah and his companions would argue as to whether the mysterious power of "the talking leaf" was a gift from the Great Spirit to the white man, or the white man's own discovery.

Sequoyah's companions had seen white men with books and had seen them write messages on paper. They were convinced that this form of communication was just another of those blessings that the Great Spirit had seen fit to bestow upon the white man but not upon the red. But Sequoyah strenuously maintained the opposite: that the Great Spirit had had nothing to do with it; and that the white man had himself invented "the talking leaf." It was an argument that remained fixed in his mind and continued to haunt him with its possibilities.

Sequoyah was born about 1770, most probably the son of a white trader named Nathaniel Gist. Nobody dwelt much on these matters of little significance. The important facts were that his mother was a member of the family of the Emperor Moytoy and the **legendary** warrior-king Oconostota; that Sequoyah was born in the Indian village of Taskigi (later Tuskegee), just five miles from the sacred town of Echota; and that he was a Cherokee. He became a craftsman in silverwork, an accomplished storyteller, and a happy participant in the Green Corn Dances, footraces, and ball games. And, along with his entire tribe, he was **illiterate**.

Sequoyah's life might have continued without incident had not a hunting accident left him partially crippled. As a result, he had more **leisure** and more opportunity to **ponder** the idea that the red man also might come to possess the secret of "the talking leaf." He began to wander off into the woods and spend hours there alone, avoiding everyone, playing like a child with pieces of wood or making odd little marks with one stone on another. His wife and friends offered no encouragement, or even **sympathy**, for they were convinced that he was either going mad or in communication with the spirits.

Months became years, and lack of sympathy became **ridicule** and **contempt**. But Sequoyah was obsessed with his dream.

At first, Sequoyah tried to give every word a separate character, but eventually he realized the **futility** of such an approach and settled on assigning a character to each sound. When his friends and neighbors talked, he no longer heard what they said but listened to the sounds, trying to separate them and trying to identify any new sound that he might theretofore have missed. What he eventually achieved was not so much an alphabet as a syllabary — 86 characters representing all the sounds of spoken Cherokee — which when combined produced a written language of remarkable simplicity and effectiveness. It had taken twelve years.

There are many stories of how Sequoyah presented his "alphabet" to his doubting people and overcame their reluctance to try it. According to one legend, there was actually a great **demonstration** before the chiefs during which his little daughter read aloud what the chiefs had privately told him to write on a paper and thus in a single moment amazed and convinced everyone. So beautifully simple and precise was Sequoyah's alphabet that it could be learned in a few days. **Moreover**, whoever learned, taught; until suddenly a most remarkable thing had happened. Within a matter of months, a population that had been almost entirely illiterate suddenly became almost entirely literate! And the same little man who had been ridiculed by his people was now respected, revered, regarded as almost superhuman and a great benefactor.

But even then Sequoyah could not rest. According to tradition, a band of Cherokees migrated west of the Mississippi at just about the time that Sequoyah was born. Where were they now, these lost Cherokees who did not know of his alphabet or the new Nation? Sequoyah, now aged, set off with a party of nine horsemen and headed south. Legend has it that before he died, somewhere deep in Mexico, he did find the lost Cherokees. Not long afterward that genus of California redwoods that included the largest trees in the world was named "sequoia" after the only man in history to conceive and perfect in its entirety an alphabet or syllabary.

From "Sequoyah" in <u>Word People</u>, by Nancy Caldwell Sorel

★ Go back to the story. Underline any words or sentences that give you clues to the meanings of the **boldfaced** words. ★

CONTEXT CLUES

In each sentence a word or phrase is underlined. Choose a word from the box to replace that word or phrase. Write it on the line.

ponder	sympathy	ridicule	legendary
leisure	illiterate	demonstration	Moreover
contempt	futility		

1. People who do amazing things, like Sequoyah, often become <u>larger-than-life figures about whom much is written.</u> _____

2. Sequoyah's greatest contribution was to make sure that future generations of Cherokees would not be <u>unable to read and write.</u> _____

3. But like many inventors, Sequoyah had to withstand <u>teasing words intended to make him look foolish</u> before people accepted his invention. _____

4. Sadly, people often look upon inventors with <u>scorn</u> because they do not understand their new ideas. _____

5. Inventors must fight the feeling of <u>uselessness</u> when others make fun of their ideas. _____

6. Fortunately, most inventors seem able to block out the doubts of others and to spend their work and <u>free-time</u> moments on creating their inventions. _____

7. They <u>think over</u> different ways to perfect their inventions. _____

8. Eventually, a few people may have <u>an understanding and a sharing of feelings</u> for the inventor's hard work and hardships and show their support. _____

9. <u>In addition</u>, they may urge others to give the invention a chance. _____

10. Then, a <u>tryout or show</u> of the invention can be held, and they hope it will be successful! _____

WORD DESCRIPTIONS

Read each word description. Then write the word from the box that best fits each description. Refer to the Dictionary, beginning on page 133, if you need help.

illiterate	ridicule	sympathy	legendary	ponder

1. You would send a card that expresses this feeling if there was a death in a friend's family. _____

2. You would use this word to describe unkind teasing. _____

3. You would use this word to describe George Washington and many other figures from history. _____

4. You would use this word to describe what you do when you think a lot about something. _____

5. You would use this word to describe someone who cannot read. _____

REWRITING SENTENCES

Rewrite each sentence using one of the words from the box.

moreover	futility	demonstration	leisure	contempt

1. In the hours when he is not working, my father likes to read.

_____

2. I miss her, and, also, I cannot find another friend.

_____

3. The soldiers had feelings of anger and scorn for the enemy.

_____

4. She gave a showing of how to decorate a cake.

_____

5. I feel the uselessness of trying to change your mind.

_____

GET WISE TO TESTS

Directions: Read the phrase. Look for the word or words that have the same or almost the same meaning as the boldfaced word. Mark the answer space for your choice.

Tip Always read all the answer choices. Many choices may make sense. But only one answer choice has the same or almost the same meaning as the boldfaced word.

Review

1. **significant** idea
   - Ⓐ foolish
   - Ⓑ able
   - Ⓒ important
   - Ⓓ hopeless

2. **comprehend** the thought
   - Ⓕ hear
   - Ⓖ see
   - Ⓗ like
   - Ⓙ understand

3. **benefit** others
   - Ⓐ hurt
   - Ⓑ help
   - Ⓒ amuse
   - Ⓓ behead

4. **illustrate** an idea
   - Ⓕ picture
   - Ⓖ darken
   - Ⓗ destroy
   - Ⓙ identify

5. **bifocal** glasses
   - Ⓐ one lens
   - Ⓑ two lenses
   - Ⓒ three lenses
   - Ⓓ no lens

6. **established** a school
   - Ⓕ closed
   - Ⓖ claimed
   - Ⓗ accomplished
   - Ⓙ founded

1. more **leisure**
   - Ⓐ money
   - Ⓑ letters
   - Ⓒ contempt
   - Ⓓ free time

2. showed **contempt**
   - Ⓕ pleasure
   - Ⓖ scorn
   - Ⓗ sympathy
   - Ⓙ clothes

3. faced **ridicule**
   - Ⓐ leisure
   - Ⓑ losing
   - Ⓒ teasing
   - Ⓓ reading

4. **legendary** hero
   - Ⓕ terrible
   - Ⓖ forgotten
   - Ⓗ larger-than-life
   - Ⓙ modern

5. had **sympathy** for
   - Ⓐ contempt
   - Ⓑ leisure
   - Ⓒ stories
   - Ⓓ understanding feelings

6. realized the **futility**
   - Ⓕ fun
   - Ⓖ hatred
   - Ⓗ ridicule
   - Ⓙ uselessness

7. great **demonstration**
   - Ⓐ show
   - Ⓑ friendship
   - Ⓒ stations
   - Ⓓ determination

8. **ponder** the idea
   - Ⓕ think about
   - Ⓖ forget about
   - Ⓗ pretend to know
   - Ⓙ borrow from

9. **moreover**, he knew
   - Ⓐ however
   - Ⓑ still
   - Ⓒ but
   - Ⓓ in addition

10. **illiterate** person
    - Ⓕ cannot speak
    - Ⓖ cannot read or write
    - Ⓗ cannot think
    - Ⓙ cannot swim

Writing

Sequoyah believed that he could create an alphabet like the white man's. He continued to believe in his idea, even when his own people made him the object of ridicule. Eventually he was successful, and the other Cherokees learned his alphabet.

Think about a time when you or someone you have heard of faced a similar situation. Write a paragraph describing what happened. Try to explain why others did not support the idea. Use some vocabulary words in your writing.

_____

_____

_____

_____

_____

_____

_____

_____

Turn to "My Personal Word List" on page 131. Write some words from the story or other words that you would like to know more about. Use a dictionary to find the meanings.

_____

_____

_____

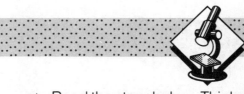

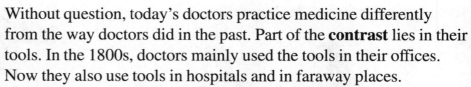

★ Read the story below. Think about the meanings of the **boldfaced** words. ★

Modern Medicine Men and Women

Without question, today's doctors practice medicine differently from the way doctors did in the past. Part of the **contrast** lies in their tools. In the 1800s, doctors mainly used the tools in their offices. Now they also use tools in hospitals and in faraway places.

In addition, many of the tools themselves are **distinctly** different from those used in the past. Some new tools measure electricity. The electrocardiograph (ECG or EKG) measures **electrical** activity of the heart. The electroencephalograph (EEG) measures electrical activity of the brain. Other inventions use sound waves and magnetic force.

Today's doctors also use computers. Computers allow doctors in different cities to work together to help the same patient. Here's how it works. The doctor who is with the patient has a **portable** camera. The doctor picks up and moves the camera to the patient. The **electron** beams of the camera pick up information. The information is fed into a computer that is connected to a telephone line. The other doctors then see the problem on their computer screens. The **visual** information helps each doctor decide how to help the patient. The patient receives the advice of several doctors but goes to only one office!

Electronic medical tools are also being used in other ways. Students who use wheelchairs need to move around safely in school. Scientists in Oregon have been able to **devise** a way for people in wheelchairs to explore new places. The students wear helmets with special glasses that have little screens. Pictures play on the **miniature** screens. The helmets also have **earphones** through which students hear sounds. Students have the **illusion** that they are really in a school. By moving joysticks on their chair arms, students can imagine moving around the school.

Medicine and the electronic age make a good mix. Doctors have wonderful new tools. They can also see patients near and far. These medical advances help doctors save more and more lives.

★ Go back to the story. Underline the words or sentences that give you a clue to the meaning of each **boldfaced** word. ★

CONTEXT CLUES

Read each sentence. Look for clues to help you complete each sentence with a word from the box. Write the word on the line.

miniature	visual	illusion	portable
electrical	devise	contrast	earphones
distinctly	electron		

1. The practice of medicine is _____ different from the way it was in the past.

2. Doctors can use movable, or _____, cameras to send information about their patients to other doctors.

3. Doctors can find out about how the heart works by reading charts that show its _____ activity.

4. There is a great _____ between the medical tools used today and those used in the past.

5. Cameras provide doctors with _____ messages so that they can see possible health problems.

6. Movable cameras have _____ beams that photograph a patient.

7. Today's health-care workers have been able to _____ ways to help wheelchair users get around in new places.

8. Students in wheelchairs can wear special helmets with _____ that send sounds to the students.

9. These helmets also allow students to see little floor plans on _____ screens built into the headsets.

10. The images give students the _____ that they are moving about in a real-life situation, preparing them for what they may really experience!

43

ANTONYMS

Remember that **antonyms** are words that have opposite meanings.
Match the words in the box with their antonyms below. Write each
word on the line.

miniature	distinctly	portable

1. vaguely _____

2. immovable _____

3. huge _____

DICTIONARY SKILLS

Each numbered example has two parts. Answer the first part by
writing a word from the box. Answer the second part by circling
the correct choice. Use the **pronunciation key** in the Dictionary to
help you.

electrical	contrast	electron
devise	distinctly	illusion

1. Write the correct spelling of di vīz′. _____
   It means **a.** invent   **b.** destroy

2. Write the correct spelling of i lek′tron. _____
   It means **a.** a kind of car   **b.** a kind of beam

3. Write the correct spelling of kon′ trast. _____
   It means **a.** a difference   **b.** a similarity

4. Write the correct spelling of i lü′zhen. _____
   It is **a.** a trick   **b.** a dance

5. Write the correct spelling of di stingkt′le _____
   It means **a.** noisily   **b.** definitely

6. Write the correct meaning of i lek′tri kəl _____
   It has to do with **a.** a city   **b.** electricity

Directions: Mark the space for the letter of the word that best completes the sentence.

 Tip If you are not sure which word best completes the sentence, do the best you can. Try to choose the answer that makes the most sense.

1. Objects that are **distinctly** different are _____ different.
   - Ⓐ little
   - Ⓒ hardly
   - Ⓑ definitely
   - Ⓓ closely

2. **Electron** beams on television carry _____.
   - Ⓕ cameras
   - Ⓗ pictures
   - Ⓖ radios
   - Ⓙ earphones

3. A **contrast** is a kind of _____.
   - Ⓐ device
   - Ⓒ similarity
   - Ⓑ contract
   - Ⓓ difference

4. Something **portable** is an item you can _____.
   - Ⓕ break
   - Ⓗ wash
   - Ⓖ carry
   - Ⓙ hear

5. Something you **devise** is something you _____.
   - Ⓐ divide
   - Ⓒ create
   - Ⓑ purchase
   - Ⓓ borrow

6. An **illusion** is a kind of _____.
   - Ⓕ trick
   - Ⓗ reality
   - Ⓖ tool
   - Ⓙ paint

7. **Earphones** are used for _____.
   - Ⓐ viewing
   - Ⓒ listening
   - Ⓑ reading
   - Ⓓ swimming

8. A **visual** display can be _____.
   - Ⓕ hidden
   - Ⓗ broken
   - Ⓖ picked
   - Ⓙ seen

9. Something **miniature** is _____.
   - Ⓐ tiny
   - Ⓒ large
   - Ⓑ lazy
   - Ⓓ lovely

10. Something **electrical** uses _____.
    - Ⓕ batteries
    - Ⓗ film
    - Ⓖ electricity
    - Ⓙ television

Review

1. An **illiterate** person is unable to _____.
   - Ⓐ read
   - Ⓒ bicycle
   - Ⓑ speak
   - Ⓓ paint

2. **Leisure** time is _____ time.
   - Ⓕ study
   - Ⓗ free
   - Ⓖ practical
   - Ⓙ busy

3. **Sympathy** is a _____.
   - Ⓐ tea
   - Ⓒ food
   - Ⓑ book
   - Ⓓ feeling

4. A **demonstration** is a kind of _____.
   - Ⓕ exercise
   - Ⓗ practice
   - Ⓖ science
   - Ⓙ show

Writing

New tools in the field of medicine have saved many lives. Computers and cameras are only a few inventions that enable doctors to treat their patients more effectively.

On the lines below, write a short story about a doctor in the future. What kinds of inventions does your doctor now have to treat his or her patients? How does the doctor use this technology in his or her practice? Use some vocabulary words in your writing.

Turn to "My Personal Word List" on page 131. Write some words from the story or other words that you would like to know more about. Use a dictionary to find the meanings.

★ Read the story below. Think about the meanings of the **boldfaced** words. ★

The Genius Machine

Today's computers are amazing machines. They are easy enough for a child to use and **manipulate**. They are also small enough to sit on a desk or on your lap. You can even have **access** to a computer in a car or an airplane! This was not always true, however. The first computers, made more than 40 years ago, were quite different.

The ENIAC (Electronic Numerical Integrator and Computer), built during World War II, was one of the first modern computers. It was an **electronic** machine that did its work by means of electricity, not mechanical switches. It took up 3,000 square feet and weighed 30 tons. It was not exactly something you would want in your lap! While today's computers have very few moving parts, the ENIAC had 6,000 switches.

About the only thing the ENIAC had in common with today's computers was its purpose. Both were meant to do tasks **automatically**, without the help of people. But the **capability**, or power, of ENIAC was limited. It could do only mathematical problems. Computers today can do everything from storytelling to household tasks. They can **monitor** many things, checking anything from a person's heart rate to the workings of a space shuttle.

Some modern computers can perform tens of millions of operations in a second and take more than 100,000,000 instructions – a seemingly **limitless** number – in the same amount of time. Today's computers also have greater **storage** capabilities. That means the computer's memory can hold more information. Now computers have the ability to process a huge **quantity** of information – billions of bits of information per minute. Compare that to the old ENIAC that took seconds to provide just one piece of information!

In its day, the ENIAC was a faster **alternative** to the human brain for working with numbers. Today's genius machines help people in ways not even thought possible in the days of ENIAC.

★ Go back to the story. Underline the words or sentences that give you a clue to the meaning of each **boldfaced** word. ★

CONTEXT CLUES

In each sentence, one word is underlined. That word sounds silly in the sentence. Choose a word from the box that can replace the silly word. Write it on the line.

electronic	access	automatically	capability
manipulate	storage	quantity	alternative
monitor	limitless		

1. Today, computers of all shapes and sizes, at home or in an office, can perform a number of difficult tasks quickly and <u>twinkles</u>. _____

2. The programs that a computer keeps in <u>rodeo</u> allow it to perform its many different functions. _____

3. Often, a special command allows the user <u>picnic</u> to these programs. _____

4. Today's computers, run by <u>playful</u> parts, are easy and inexpensive for an individual to operate.

    _____

5. You would be surprised at the <u>mosquito</u> tasks a home computer can perform by pressing just a few keys. _____

6. A home computer has the <u>sideways</u> to do household tasks. _____

7. One family uses its home computer to calculate and <u>shriek</u> its daily expenses. _____

8. Another family collects a large <u>lizard</u> of computer games for home entertainment. _____

9. Good instructions can help someone easily <u>sneeze</u> most computer parts correctly within a short period of time. _____

10. Do you think a future <u>measles</u> to the computer will be invented sometime soon? _____

SYNONYMS

Remember that **synonyms** are words that have the same or almost the same meaning. Write a word from the box that is a synonym of the underlined word in each sentence.

quantity	capability	limitless
monitor	manipulate	

1. The <u>power</u> of a computer made several years ago is nowhere

   near the _____ of a computer now.

2. Today, uses for computers are almost as <u>endless</u> as the

   seemingly _____ instructions they can handle.

3. Computers can be told to <u>check</u> the workings of a space shuttle

   and _____ a person's heart rate.

4. Computers can remember a great <u>amount</u> of information and

   print out a huge _____ of it in seconds.

5. Yet computers can be so easy to <u>use</u> that children can

   _____ them without a problem.

CLOZE PARAGRAPH

Use the words in the box to complete the passage. Reread the passage to be sure it makes sense.

automatically	storage	alternatives
electronic	access	

   In order to (1) _____ a computer program, you need to know the commands that will help you gain entry. Once you are in a program, the computer can perform tasks

(2) _____. Many programs have a menu that offers

(3) _____. Information that is entered can be put in

(4) _____ so that it can be recalled later on. A

computer is indeed a marvelous (5)_____ machine, once it is plugged in and turned on!

WORD MAP

Use the vocabulary words in the box to complete the word map about modern computers. Add other words that you know to each group. One heading will not have any vocabulary words, but only your words.

electronic	storage	capability	automatically
monitor	limitless	quantity	access

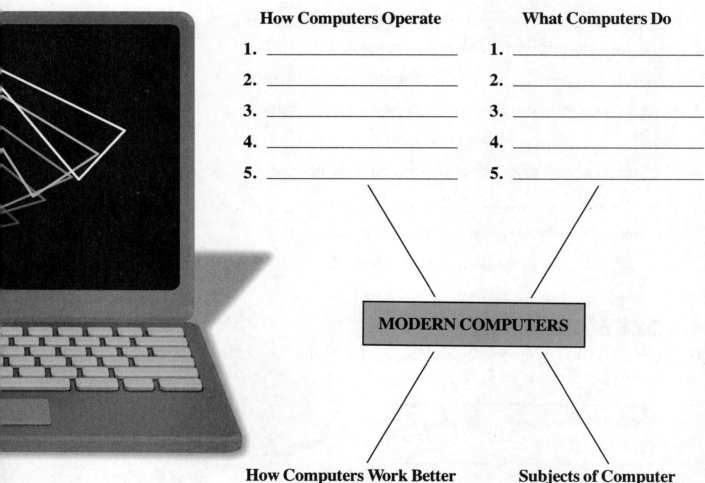

How Computers Operate

1. _____
2. _____
3. _____
4. _____
5. _____

What Computers Do

1. _____
2. _____
3. _____
4. _____
5. _____

MODERN COMPUTERS

How Computers Work Better Than People

1. _____
2. _____
3. _____
4. _____
5. _____

Subjects of Computer Games

1. _____
2. _____
3. _____
4. _____
5. _____

GET WISE TO TESTS

Directions: Read the sentences. Look for the best word to use in the blank. Mark the answer space for your choice.

Tip

Some tests have letters inside the answer circles. Fill in the circle next to your answer, covering the letter, too.

---

1. The computers were locked up in the basement. So no one had _____ to them.
   - Ⓐ storage
   - Ⓒ access
   - Ⓑ alternative
   - Ⓓ answers

2. A computer's power source is electricity. It is an _____ machine.
   - Ⓕ absolute
   - Ⓗ covered
   - Ⓖ electronic
   - Ⓙ impossible

3. The first computer could only do math problems. It had limited _____.
   - Ⓐ capability
   - Ⓒ gasoline
   - Ⓑ quantity
   - Ⓓ price

4. This is a vacuum cleaner. It is a modern-day _____ to a broom.
   - Ⓕ handle
   - Ⓗ access
   - Ⓖ element
   - Ⓙ alternative

5. Information entered in a computer can be saved. Computers are _____ machines.
   - Ⓐ quantity
   - Ⓒ storage
   - Ⓑ number
   - Ⓓ absence

6. Computers have changed our lives. They have _____ possibilities.
   - Ⓕ helpless
   - Ⓗ thick
   - Ⓖ limitless
   - Ⓙ fortunate

7. Give proper commands to a computer. Watch it do the tasks _____.
   - Ⓐ hopelessly
   - Ⓒ playfully
   - Ⓑ sadly
   - Ⓓ automatically

8. There are enough games for everyone. There is an endless _____ of them at the store.
   - Ⓕ quantity
   - Ⓗ access
   - Ⓖ price
   - Ⓙ gratitude

9. Computers help doctors watch patients. The machines _____ heart rate, pulse, and other bodily functions.
   - Ⓐ multiply
   - Ⓒ manipulate
   - Ⓑ gasp
   - Ⓓ monitor

10. Many computers are easy to use. A person with little training can easily _____ them.
   - Ⓕ dampen
   - Ⓗ manipulate
   - Ⓖ monitor
   - Ⓙ bathe

Review

1. My _____ radio is light. It is easy to carry.
   - Ⓐ breakable
   - Ⓒ artificial
   - Ⓑ portable
   - Ⓓ enormous

2. He has a _____ camera in his pocket. He takes many pictures.
   - Ⓕ huge
   - Ⓗ busy
   - Ⓖ visual
   - Ⓙ miniature

Writing

The ENIAC was an amazing machine for its time. What do you think the computers of the future will be like? Pretend that you are an inventor who has just completed work on a totally new kind of computer.

Write a paragraph describing your invention. Tell what it looks like and what it does. Think about how your invention can help make the lives of people better, and include those thoughts in your paragraph. Use some vocabulary words in your writing.

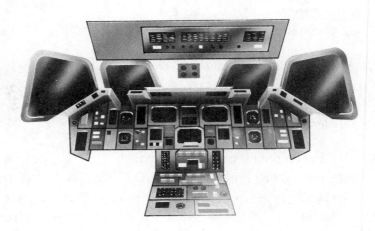

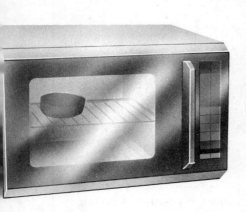

Turn to "My Personal Word List" on page 131. Write some words from the story or other words that you would like to know more about. Use a dictionary to find the meanings.

★ To review the words in Lessons 5–8, turn to page 126. ★

THE OLYMPIC DREAM

Everyone loves to win. But some athletes have what it takes to set themselves apart from the rest. What makes them special?

In Lessons 9–12, you will read about the Olympic games. You will meet some athletes who have sought a gold medal and won it. How do you think an Olympic athlete prepares for this tough competition? How might each athlete feel as he or she steps into the spotlight? Write your ideas on the lines below.

Preparing to Compete	**Feelings About the Olympics**
_____	_____
_____	_____
_____	_____
_____	_____
_____	_____

★ Read the story below. Think about the meanings of the **boldfaced** words. ★

For the Glory of Zeus

The next time you watch an Olympic race, think about Coroebus. This young runner was the first Olympic winner on record. He won a two-hundred-meter race held near a place called Olympia, in Greece. That was three thousand years ago.

The Olympic games were started as part of a religious ceremony, a **tribute** to the chief Greek god, Zeus. They were held every four years. At first, there was only one event, the race that Coroebus won. People came from neighboring villages to sit on the grass and watch. Later, a **stadium** was built. Then the runners competed in this enclosed, roofless area.

As the games become more popular, events were added. These included chariot races and the pentathlon. This five-event contest featured running, jumping, wrestling, throwing the discus, and throwing the **javelin**, or spear.

At the height of the games in ancient Greece, **attendance** was in the tens of thousands. Only men could go to the games. Women were not permitted to watch, and any found at the games could be put to death. The men at the Olympics came from all over the Greek world. During times of war, they would **proclaim** a truce during and just after the games. With peace declared, men could travel without fear.

Then, as now, the athletes underwent **strenuous** training. Every day they worked out under the stern eyes of coaches. They were also very **competitive**. Winning was everything. It was the **supreme** achievement. No prizes were given for second or third place. Losers walked away in shame.

With great **pomp** and splendor, each winning player was marched to the Temple of Zeus. There, the **contestant** received his prize, a wreath from the sacred olive tree. But the most important prize for an Olympic athlete was the honor of being the best, earned through great skill and effort.

★ Go back to the story. Underline the words or sentences that give you a clue to the meaning of each **boldfaced** word. ★

CONTEXT CLUES

Read each sentence. Look for clues to help you complete each sentence with a word from the box. Write the word on the line.

pomp	strenuous	supreme	proclaim
tribute	competitive	javelin	attendance
stadium	contestant		

1. The Greeks honored Zeus, their chief god, by paying

   _____ to him through athletic events at Olympic games.

2. The Olympic events required a lot of energy; in fact, they were

   so _____ that only the strongest and most skilled had even a small chance to win.

3. The athletes competed in an enclosed area, a roofless building

   called a _____.

4. The Olympic games became so popular that the stadium was

   always filled, with _____ in the tens of thousands.

5. People's everyday lives were ordinary, so they loved the

   excitement created by the _____ and ceremony of the Olympics.

6. Throwing the _____, or spear, was a part of a tough five-event contest.

7. Each _____ had to perform well in all five events in order to win.

8. Each athlete was very _____ because winning was most important.

9. To win was the _____ achievement; to lose meant shame.

10. Overall, the Olympic games meant so much to the people

    of ancient Greece that they would _____ a truce during a time of war in order to hold the games.

ANALOGIES

Remember that an **analogy** compares two pairs of words. The relationship between the first pair of words is the same as the relationship between the second pair of words. Use the words in the box to complete the following analogies.

stadium	contestant	proclaim
supreme	strenuous	
tribute	javelin	

1. Smallest is to least as highest is to _____.

2. Game is to player as contest is to _____.

3. Question is to ask as statement is to _____.

4. Roof is to building as sky is to _____.

5. Swing is to bat as throw is to _____.

6. Mistreat is to insult as honor is to _____.

7. Inactive is to sluggish as active is to _____.

CLOZE PARAGRAPH

Use the words in the box to complete the passage. Then reread the passage to be sure it makes sense.

strenuous	pomp	competitive
attendance	stadium	

If you wanted to compete as an athlete in the Olympic games,

you would have to go through (1) _____ training.

You would have to be very (2) _____ in order to

win. Or you might just enjoy watching the Olympic games with all

their splendor and (3) _____. Just being in

(4) _____ could be truly exciting. I have never sat

in an Olympic (5) _____, but I hope to have that
experience someday.

WORD MAP

Use the vocabulary words in the box to complete the word map about both ancient and modern Olympic games. Add other words that you know to each group.

contestants	tribute	stadium
competitive	strenuous	javelin

Why Held

1. _____

2. _____

3. _____

Where Held

1. _____

2. _____

3. _____

OLYMPIC GAMES

Who Is There

1. _____

2. _____

3. _____

4. _____

5. _____

6. _____

Kinds of Events

1. _____

2. _____

3. _____

4. _____

5. _____

6. _____

GET WISE TO TESTS

Directions: Read each sentence. Pick the word that best completes the sentence. Mark the answer space for that word.

Before you choose an answer, try reading the sentences with each answer choice. This will help you choose an answer that makes sense.

Review

1. I hope the computer is working. I need to _____ a file.
   Ⓐ research
   Ⓑ available
   Ⓒ access
   Ⓓ manipulate

2. Now that we missed the movie, we will have to think of an _____.
   Ⓕ actively
   Ⓖ exercised
   Ⓗ automatically
   Ⓙ alternative

3. We bought a new refrigerator that makes ice _____.
   Ⓐ automatically
   Ⓑ freezer
   Ⓒ watering
   Ⓓ access

4. My hands are so cold, I can hardly _____ this pen to write my name.
   Ⓕ mastered
   Ⓖ manipulate
   Ⓗ working
   Ⓙ alternative

1. The crowd was impressed by the _____ of the ceremony.
   Ⓐ pomp
   Ⓑ their
   Ⓒ fortunately
   Ⓓ proclaim

2. In her speech, the winner paid _____ to her coach.
   Ⓕ exhausting
   Ⓖ stadium
   Ⓗ lengthen
   Ⓙ tribute

3. The judges will _____ the winners.
   Ⓐ additional
   Ⓑ proclaim
   Ⓒ countless
   Ⓓ javelin

4. The _____ are lined up for the race.
   Ⓕ volunteering
   Ⓖ thrashed
   Ⓗ contestants
   Ⓙ attendance

5. Some of the races are very _____ and tiring.
   Ⓐ supreme
   Ⓑ strenuous
   Ⓒ according
   Ⓓ enjoyment

6. The large _____ holds 50,000 people.
   Ⓕ supreme
   Ⓖ devour
   Ⓗ stadium
   Ⓙ another

7. The bad weather caused poor _____ at the events.
   Ⓐ competitive
   Ⓑ attendance
   Ⓒ jealousy
   Ⓓ established

8. Watch how far that man can throw the _____.
   Ⓕ agreeable
   Ⓖ strenuous
   Ⓗ undo
   Ⓙ javelin

9. A gold medal is a _____ achievement.
   Ⓐ stadium
   Ⓑ admiration
   Ⓒ supreme
   Ⓓ narrator

10. There is a _____ spirit among the national teams.
    Ⓕ delivery
    Ⓖ contestant
    Ⓗ disguise
    Ⓙ competitive

Writing

In the story, you learned that winning was everything to the athletes at the ancient Olympic games. Athletes who take part in today's Olympics point out the importance of meeting new people, sharing experiences, the spirit of friendship, and the privilege of just being able to compete. If you were competing in the Olympics, what would be most important to you?

Write a paragraph expressing your view. The pictures may help you develop some ideas. Use some vocabulary words in your writing.

_____

_____

_____

_____

_____

_____

_____

_____

_____

_____

_____

_____

_____

Turn to "My Personal Word List" on page 132. Write some words from the story or other words that you would like to know more about. Use a dictionary to find the meanings.

_____

_____

_____

_____

★ Read the story below. Think about the meanings of the **boldfaced** words. ★

The Will to Win

What is it that helps a winner win? Al Oerter, trying for his third Olympic gold medal, has the determination to overcome his injury.

On the 15th day of October, 1964, big Al Oerter, two-time Olympic discus-throwing champion, walked stiffly onto the **infield** of the great Olympic stadium in Tokyo. Carefully, almost **clumsily**, he moved toward the **discus** circle, his face grim. And none of the spectators knew what an impossible test of courage lay before this man.

Only a week ago he had been strongly confident of his ability to win, for the third time, an Olympic gold medal. He had felt the excitement of settling into the Olympic Village with the United States team, of meeting old friends and new competitors from other nations, swapping stories and track records, of checking the superb **facilities** of the costly new stadium.

But then opening day had come, the sky clear blue, the sun polished to brilliance for the occasion. At the stroke of one that Saturday, a burst of music sounded through the stadium. One band, then another and another came through the entrance chutes.

And then came the most dramatic moment: the arrival of the Olympic flame. The flame is always kindled at Olympia in Greece and, no matter how far or how difficult, a **host** of relay runners carry it by land, by sea, by air to the scene of the Olympics.

The next day the competition began, and records started falling almost immediately. But for Al Oerter, it looked as though he were finished without even an appearance.

In a practice throw the **husky** 28-year-old from Long Island had ripped the **cartilage** off his rib cage. He knew without being told that the injury was serious, but he did not learn how serious until the American team physicians, Dr. Harry McPhee and Dr. Dan Hanley, checked him over.

They shook their heads. "It's going to take at least a month for that injury to heal," they told him.

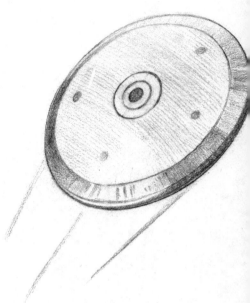

They taped him up and told him to stay quiet. But Al's fighting spirit wouldn't give up. It was impossible to throw the discus in his condition — but he knew he was going to do it. And he made his announcement to the doctors.

They were flatly against him. "You'll **hemorrhage**," they warned. "You can't stand the pain."

"I'll stand it," he told them.

At last they gave their **reluctant** permission. The sixth day of the Games came — the day Al Oerter had to compete. The doctors strapped a clumsy jacket on Al, hoping that the ice it was filled with would slow down the hemorrhaging.

He moved out to the field. Al got off his first throw. It was low and short, and the pain that cut through him nearly ripped him in two. Sweat popped out on his face. It took every ounce of effort he had to keep from showing his agony.

Somebody put a blanket around him. He huddled under it, **hoarding** his strength. The time for his second throw came, and it, too, was low. The pain was red hot. He faced the third of his six throws and he almost quit, but he wouldn't. The throw was no good. Neither was his fourth throw.

He had only two chances left. It looked hopeless. He could quit now. Nobody would blame him. He had tried harder than anybody would ever expect him to — anybody but himself.

Silently, he gave himself a pep talk. "You can do it," he said. "You don't have to give up. This is the Olympics. Get in there and stretch one."

And he did. Shutting his mind to everything except the one thing he wanted — to get that discus out there — he stepped into the circle, crouched, whirled, and got one off. It sailed 200 feet 1 1/2 inches for an Olympic record. Al Oerter had made it.

And when it was all over, and the gold medal was his, he said to the newspaper men clustering around him: "Don't make me a hero. I wanted to win so I gutted it out."

The will to win! Name every Olympic champion, this is one quality they all share. They *want* to make it.

From Olympic Champions: Why They Win, by Carli Laklan

★ Go back to the story. Underline any words or sentences that give you clues to the meanings of the **boldfaced** words. ★

CONTEXT CLUES

Read each sentence. Look for clues to help you complete each sentence with a word from the box. Write the word on the line.

reluctant	hoarding	husky	clumsily
cartilage	discus	infield	hemorrhage
facilities	host		

1. In 1964 Al Oerter was already a two-time champion at throwing the _____, and he was hoping to win an Olympic gold medal for the third time.

2. Oerter's _____ frame had helped him become a powerful discus-thrower.

3. The costly _____ where the athletes trained and competed were built especially for the 1964 Olympic games in Tokyo, Japan.

4. Practice for the discus-throwing event took place at the _____ of the track.

5. After the accident, Oerter moved awkwardly and _____ over to the doctors to be examined.

6. He knew his injury was serious when he learned that the _____, the connective tissue, had been ripped away from his rib cage.

7. Doctors put an ice-filled jacket on Oerter, hoping that it would help stop the flow of blood in case he started to _____.

8. A _____ of fans cheered for Oerter as he threw the discus while trying not to let the agony he was feeling show on his face.

9. Oerter was _____, or storing up, his strength between throws by relaxing and keeping his body warm.

10. He was _____, or hesitant, to speak to reporters because he didn't want them to turn him into a hero.

WORD ORIGINS

Knowing the origin of a word can help you understand its meaning. Read each word origin. Then write each word from the box next to its origin.

hoarding	infield	reluctant	discus
hemorrhage	cartilage	clumsily	facilities

1. from Old English disc, plate _____

2. from Old English feld, floor; area _____

3. from Greek haimorrhagia, with blood _____

4. from Latin facilitās, to do _____

5. from Old English hord, to hide away _____

6. from Latin reluctari, struggle _____

7. from Latin cartilāgō, gristle, tissue _____

8. from Middle English clumsen and Swedish klumsig, stiff, awkward _____

MULTIPLE MEANINGS

The words in the box have more than one meaning. Look for clues in each sentence to tell which meaning is used. Write the letter of the meaning next to the correct sentence.

husky	host
a. big and strong in body	**a.** person who entertains a guest
b. hoarse in voice	**b.** head of a TV show
c. an arctic sled dog	**c.** a large amount or number

____ 1. She spoke in a husky voice.

____ 2. The husky barked loudly.

____ 3. He is a husky man.

____ 4. He will host the TV show.

____ 5. I am the host of the party.

____ 6. A host of people arrived late for the party.

GET WISE TO TESTS

Directions: Read the phrase. Look for the word or words that have the same or almost the same meaning as the boldfaced word. Mark the answer space for your choice.

Tip

This test will show how well you understand the meaning of words. Think about the meaning of the boldfaced word before you choose your answer.

Review

1. **miniature** house
   - (A) rented
   - (B) painted
   - (C) huge
   - (D) tiny

2. make a **prediction**
   - (F) forecast
   - (G) movement
   - (H) diagram
   - (J) commotion

3. throw the **javelin**
   - (A) record
   - (B) stadium
   - (C) spear
   - (D) pomp

4. **supreme** achievement
   - (F) careless
   - (G) highest
   - (H) busy
   - (J) strenuous

5. quite a **contrast**
   - (A) wireless
   - (B) contest
   - (C) picture
   - (D) difference

1. **reluctant** answer
   - (A) quick
   - (B) vague
   - (C) clear
   - (D) hesitant

2. **hoarding** food
   - (F) preparing
   - (G) eating
   - (H) storing up
   - (J) throwing away

3. toss the **discus**
   - (A) dish
   - (B) square board
   - (C) disk
   - (D) key

4. a **host** of people
   - (F) small group
   - (G) guest
   - (H) choice
   - (J) large number

5. **husky** man
   - (A) small and thin
   - (B) big and strong
   - (C) interesting
   - (D) professional

6. **clumsily** thrown
   - (F) awkwardly
   - (G) superbly
   - (H) accurately
   - (J) carefully

7. torn **cartilage**
   - (A) dark fabric
   - (B) colored paper
   - (C) rough material
   - (D) connective tissue

8. excellent **facilities**
   - (F) instructors
   - (G) buildings
   - (H) events
   - (J) medals

9. near the **infield**
   - (A) area inside the track
   - (B) field on a farm
   - (C) place in a garden
   - (D) part of the body

10. stop the **hemorrhage**
    - (F) sewing
    - (G) crying
    - (H) bleeding
    - (J) throwing

Writing

Even though Al Oerter knew he had a serious injury, he went on to compete. He not only risked further injury and hemorrhaging, he also could have caused permanent damage to his body. Should Al Oerter have done this? Do you think that winning a medal is worth risking your health?

Write a paragraph expressing your point of view. Use some vocabulary words in your writing.

_____

_____

_____

_____

_____

_____

_____

_____

_____

_____

_____

_____

_____

_____

_____

_____

_____

_____

_____

Turn to "My Personal Word List" on page 132. Write some words from the story or other words that you would like to know more about. Use a dictionary to find the meanings.

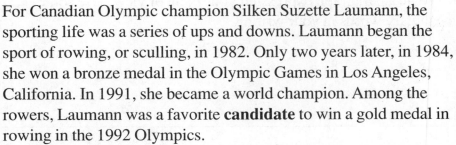

★ Read the story below. Think about the meanings of
the **boldfaced** words. ★

The Comeback Kid

For Canadian Olympic champion Silken Suzette Laumann, the
sporting life was a series of ups and downs. Laumann began the
sport of rowing, or sculling, in 1982. Only two years later, in 1984,
she won a bronze medal in the Olympic Games in Los Angeles,
California. In 1991, she became a world champion. Among the
rowers, Laumann was a favorite **candidate** to win a gold medal in
rowing in the 1992 Olympics.

In May of 1992, however, Laumann was injured. She was
practicing for a race in Germany when another boat crashed into hers.
The impact broke Laumann's ankle and tore several leg muscles.
Even after five operations, doctors thought Laumann might not ever
be able to row again. They certainly did not expect that she would
be **capable** of competing in the Barcelona Olympics in August.

Laumann surprised everyone with her quick recovery. One
important part of her comeback was her determination to get well.
Another important **factor** was that she began exercising while still
in her hospital bed. Most rowers train with weight lifting and **cross-
country** running. Laumann could not run, but she could exercise
her arms. By August, using a cane and a leg brace, Laumann was
able to compete in Barcelona. She had **attained** her goal of
recovering in time for the Olympics.

In the race, Laumann rowed her scull against one other scull.
Rowers must be able to figure out how fast they are going. Laumann
knew she must **gauge** her speed carefully. A **stopwatch** was used
to measure the time it took each scull to reach the finish line. As the
two scullers finished the course, their times were posted on a
scoreboard.

On August 3, 1992, the Canadian **spectators** watching at home
stayed up until 3:00 A.M. to see Laumann compete. No one who
watched has ever forgotten how she rowed to the third-fastest time
and a bronze medal. Laumann won a place in the **archives** of
Olympic history – and in the hearts of all Canadians.

★ Go back to the story. Underline the words or sentences that give
you a clue to the meaning of each **boldfaced** word. ★

USING CONTEXT

Meanings for the vocabulary words are given below. Go back to the story and read each sentence that contains a vocabulary word. If you still cannot tell the meaning, look for clues in the sentences that come before and after the one with the vocabulary word. Write each word in front of its meaning.

candidate	attained	cross-country	gauge
archives	stopwatch	spectators	factor
capable	scoreboard		

1. _____: a watch that can be instantly stopped and started, used for measuring tiny amounts of time

2. _____: people who watch something or look on without taking part

3. _____: to measure something; to judge

4. _____: a board on which scores of a sporting event are posted

5. _____: person who seeks a position of honor

6. _____: going across open country such as fields and woods instead of using a road

7. _____: element or idea that helps to bring about a result

8. _____: historical records

9. _____: able; having the power, ability, and fitness to do something

10. _____: reached, achieved; gained through effort

CHALLENGE YOURSELF

Name two factors that are important to success in school.

_____   _____

Name an activity that you are capable of doing well.

_____   _____

67

WORD GROUPS

Read each pair of words. Think about how they are alike. Write the word from the box that best completes each group.

spectators	stopwatch	candidate	capable	archives

1. records, documents, _____

2. audience, fans, _____

3. clock, timer, _____ ◆ ◆ ◆

4. able, ready, _____

5. applicant, nominee, _____

REWRITING SENTENCES

Rewrite each sentence using one of the vocabulary words from the box.

cross-country	attained	gauge
scoreboard	archives	factor

1. The rower achieved her goal of finishing the race.

_____

2. The coach will carefully determine the distance.

_____

3. Joe's love of animals was a major element in his decision to become a veterinarian.

_____

4. The board showing the score proved that we won the game by a narrow margin.

_____

5. My mom's name is in the school's historical records.

_____

6. Running across open fields is one way to train for many sports.

_____

GET WISE TO TESTS

Directions: Choose the word or words that best take the place of the boldfaced word.

Always read all the answer choices. Many choices may make sense. But only one answer choice has the same or almost the same meaning as the boldfaced word.

1. She weighed many **factors** to make her decision.
   A pounds
   B elements
   C tributes
   D errors

2. The **spectators** cheered. They loved seeing a winner.
   F viewers
   G contestants
   H score
   J losers

3. The woman was a **capable** runner. She was fast!
   A scared
   B able
   C horrible
   D careful

4. Check the **archives**. All the information is there.
   F records
   G stadium
   H earphones
   J architects

5. Several sports have **cross-country** events.
   A downhill
   B uphill
   C across the countryside
   D record-breaking

6. The team **attained** victory. They worked for this goal.
   F surrendered
   G watched
   H attended
   J reached

7. She was a **candidate**. She hoped to make the team.
   A coach
   B contestant
   C manager
   D judge

8. Try to **gauge** an opponent. Figure out his strengths.
   F trick
   G ignore
   H judge
   J proclaim

9. The runner's **stopwatch** tells how fast he went.
   A wireless
   B calendar
   C stoplight
   D timer

10. Look at the **scoreboard**. Our team is winning.
    F cardboard playing field
    G board with the score
    H announcer
    J goalposts

Review

1. The dancer pretended to move **clumsily**. He really was very graceful.
   A quickly
   B awkwardly
   C slowly
   D smoothly

2. He is a **husky** boy. Maybe he will be a football player someday.
   F big and strong
   G mean and tough
   H sickly
   J athletic

3. There are a **host** of reasons why I cannot come over. Homework is just one of many.
   A category
   B small degree
   C large number
   D overflow

4. The injury caused him to **hemorrhage**. He lost a lot of blood.
   F sneeze
   G bleed
   H cry
   J hurt

69

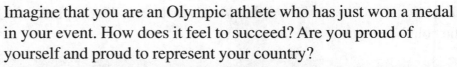

Writing

Imagine that you are an Olympic athlete who has just won a medal in your event. How does it feel to succeed? Are you proud of yourself and proud to represent your country?

On the lines below tell about what event you entered. Use the pictures to help you. Why do you like this sport? How did you train to make the Olympics? Describe what it might be like to be with other athletes from all around the world. Use some vocabulary words in your writing.

_____

_____

_____

_____

_____

_____

_____

_____

_____

_____

_____

_____

_____

_____

_____

_____

_____

_____

Turn to "My Personal Word List" on page 132. Write some words from the story or other words that you would like to know more about. Use a dictionary to find the meanings.

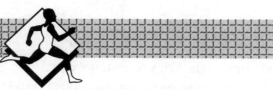

★ Read the story below. Think about the meanings of the **boldfaced** words. ★

A Heart of Gold

When Oksana Baiul stepped onto the ice, the arena was quiet. Then she smiled, and the **enthusiastic** audience applauded loudly. Baiul loved to ice skate, and it showed. Through many hard times, she kept a positive **attitude**. Her cheerful outlook helped her keep skating and winning. She won a gold medal in the 1994 Olympics when she was only 16!

Baiul worked hard at her skating. Continued **dedication** to the sport helped her overcome many difficult times in her life. Raised in the country of Ukraine, Baiul started skating at the age of 3. She was a natural on ice. She was **agile** and could easily move her body in jumps and spins. By the time Baiul was 14, her mother and grandparents had died, and her father and coach had left her. Skating became the basic, or **fundamental**, thing in her life. She would not give up.

Baiul went to live with a new coach and became part of the family. She could not afford new clothes or new skates very often, though. At one point, she used the same pair of skates for four years. However, Baiul never let hardship affect the **vitality** of her performances. Her energy and liveliness always came through. Baiul's **fervent** love of skating showed in every move. Although she was only 5'3" tall and weighed just 95 pounds, her deep feelings for skating made her seem much bigger on the ice.

On the day of the 1994 Olympic competition, Baiul attended a practice **session** with five other skaters. During the practice, a collision with another skater injured her back and cut her leg. She was weary from stress. **Fatigued** as she was, Baiul had to make a decision. Should she give up her chance for the gold because she was tired and hurt? Baiul decided not to **sacrifice** the chance. She skated a perfect routine and even added a risky jump. Her victory was the slimmest in Olympic figure-skating history. But the judges said the program came from the heart. You might say Oksana Baiul truly had a heart of "gold"!

★ Go back to the story. Underline the words or sentences that give you a clue to the meaning of each **boldfaced** word. ★

USING CONTEXT

Meanings for the vocabulary words are given below. Go back to the story and read each sentence that contains a vocabulary word. If you still cannot tell the meaning, look for clues in the sentences that come before and after the one with the vocabulary word. Write each word in front of its meaning.

enthusiastic dedication attitude	session fervent fatigued	fundamental sacrifice	agile vitality

1. _____: tired, weary

2. _____: interested and excited

3. _____: willingness to give great effort to a certain purpose

4. _____: liveliness; energy

5. _____: showing deep feeling

6. _____: basic

7. _____: state of mind; way of thinking

8. _____: a single period of time

9. _____: to give up for the sake of something else

10. _____: able to move easily and quickly

CHALLENGE YOURSELF

Name two things you are enthusiastic about.

_____   _____

Name two things that can make you feel fatigued.

_____   _____

SYNONYMS AND ANTONYMS

Remember that **synonyms** are words that have the same or nearly the same meaning. **Antonyms** are words that have opposite meanings.

Each word in the box is either a synonym or an antonym of one of the words listed below. Match each word with its synonym or antonym. Write each word on the line.

fundamental	enthusiastic	fatigued
fervent	agile	sacrifice

1. tired _____

2. stiff _____

3. unnecessary _____

4. intense _____

5. uninterested _____

6. surrender _____

MULTIPLE MEANINGS

The words in the box have more than one meaning. Look for clues in each sentence to tell which meaning is being used. Write the letter of the meaning next to the correct sentence.

dedication	session
a. willingness to give great effort to a cause	**a.** a period of time for an activity
b. an event showing special attention or respect	**b.** a part of the school year

_____ **1.** There were 500 people at the dedication of the new school.

_____ **2.** She showed great dedication when she finished all her schoolwork before going to the movie.

_____ **3.** Can you come to a practice session with the band on Saturday?

_____ **4.** My sister is planning to go to the summer session of classes at her college.

WRITING SENTENCES

Write an original sentence with each of the words in the box.

attitude	agile	session	vitality	fervent

1. _____

2. _____

3. _____

4. _____

5. _____

DICTIONARY SKILLS

Write the words in alphabetical order, one word on each line. Then turn to the Dictionary, beginning on page 133. Find each word in the Dictionary and write its meaning below.

enthusiastic sacrifice	dedication fervent	fatigued vitality	fundamental session

1. _____

2. _____

3. _____

4. _____

5. _____

6. _____

7. _____

8. _____

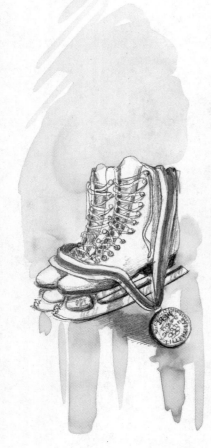

GET WISE TO TESTS

Directions: Read the sentences. Look for the best word to use in the blank. Mark the answer space for your choice.

 Read carefully. Use the other words in the sentences to help you choose each missing word.

1. Timing is important in figure skating. In fact, it is _____ to the sport.
   Ⓐ graceful   Ⓒ fundamental
   Ⓑ fervent   Ⓓ additional

2. You must make fast turns and quick jumps in figure skating. You must be _____.
   Ⓕ agile   Ⓗ fatigued
   Ⓖ ridiculous   Ⓙ alone

3. Skating was her love. She was _____ about doing well.
   Ⓐ fearful   Ⓒ fervent
   Ⓑ agile   Ⓓ supreme

4. The skaters gave up free time for their sport. It was a big _____.
   Ⓕ sacrifice   Ⓗ session
   Ⓖ resource   Ⓙ festival

5. The crowd roared as the skaters came out. It was an _____ welcome.
   Ⓐ amusing   Ⓒ eventual
   Ⓑ agile   Ⓓ enthusiastic

6. Top athletes work with real purpose. Their _____ is impressive.
   Ⓕ session   Ⓗ quantity
   Ⓖ description   Ⓙ dedication

7. After the contest, everyone was tired. The skater felt _____.
   Ⓐ fervent   Ⓒ fatigued
   Ⓑ fantastic   Ⓓ elegant

8. The coach gave helpful tips during the workout. It was a good _____.
   Ⓕ sacrifice   Ⓗ departure
   Ⓖ session   Ⓙ arrival

9. One skater did not want to work hard. This is not the right _____.
   Ⓐ sacrifice   Ⓒ rule
   Ⓑ attention   Ⓓ attitude

10. The champion skated with great energy. The crowd loved her _____.
    Ⓕ vitality   Ⓗ coach
    Ⓖ vitamins   Ⓙ pomp

Review

1. The _____ cheered. They threw their hats onto the field.
   Ⓐ sellers   Ⓒ stadium
   Ⓑ spectators   Ⓓ potatoes

2. A _____ is useful in a marathon. It times the runners.
   Ⓕ stopwatch   Ⓗ sneakers
   Ⓖ stoplight   Ⓙ radio

Writing

Think about the qualities shared by the Olympic athletes in the stories you have read. Spirit, dedication, and courage are all words that come to mind when describing these champions.

Write a paragraph about how you can apply the Olympic attitude to an area in your life. Is there something that you would like to improve, such as your schoolwork or maybe an interest outside of school? Use some vocabulary words in your writing.

_____

_____

_____

_____

_____

_____

_____

_____

_____

_____

_____

_____

_____

_____

_____

_____

_____

Turn to "My Personal Word List" on page 132. Write some words from the story or other words that you would like to know more about. Use a dictionary to find the meanings.

★ To review the words in Lessons 9–12, turn to page 127. ★

WORLD WONDERS

These Egyptian pyramids, built about 4,500 years ago, are among the Seven Wonders of the Ancient World.

In Lessons 13–16, you will read about some wonders that amaze people around the world. One is a wall nearly 4,000 miles long. Others are tombs more than 4,000 years old. Think of some amazing structures that you have seen or read about. How would you describe those wonders? Write your ideas on the lines below.

Amazing Structures	What Makes Them Amazing

★ Read the story below. Think about the meanings of the **boldfaced** words. ★

Faces in Stone

When **sculptor** Gutzon Borglum first **beheld** Mount Rushmore in the Black Hills of South Dakota, he knew he was looking at the place where he would carve his greatest work of art. "American history shall march along that skyline!" he said.

And march it did, in the shape of four **renowned** Americans, all great presidents. Borglum's sculpture on the face of the mountain shows the **bust** of George Washington. Washington's head and shoulders stand as high as a five-story building. Next to Washington are **carvings** of Thomas Jefferson, Abraham Lincoln, and Theodore Roosevelt.

The place for the Mount Rushmore Memorial was chosen in 1925. Borglum said then it would take seven years to create the artwork. In fact, the sculpture took twice that time.

Many problems slowed the progress. Right away, the start on the memorial was delayed two years for lack of money. The work was also difficult. Each of the heads was cut out of the granite cliff atop Mount Rushmore's **summit**. Borglum's crew used explosives and drills to shape the four faces on this highest point of the mountain. Sometimes mistakes were made. One big error was made in cutting Jefferson's head. It had to be blasted away and a new one begun.

Throughout the project, Borglum was **assisted** by his son, Lincoln. The boy was 12 when he started helping. He was a man of 26 when he put the finishing touches on the sculpture, just a few months after his father's death. The mighty efforts of the two Borglums had created a magnificent sculpture. The **majestic** heads of the presidents stand 60 feet tall. They make up the world's largest sculpture.

Unlike many memorials, there is no **inscription** on Mount Rushmore. Time has shown that this exciting artwork needs no words to describe it. These **dramatic** faces from American history speak for themselves.

★ Go back to the story. Underline the words or sentences that give you a clue to the meaning of each **boldfaced** word. ★

CONTEXT CLUES

In each sentence, a word or phrase is underlined. Choose a word from the box to replace that word or phrase. Write the word on the line.

renowned	sculptor	majestic	inscription
beheld	carvings	dramatic	assisted
bust	summit		

1. Each year, many tourists come to see the sculptures at Mount Rushmore. _____

2. On the left side of Mount Rushmore is a sculpture showing the head and shoulders of George Washington. _____

3. Other carvings include the famous American Presidents Thomas Jefferson, Abraham Lincoln, and Theodore Roosevelt. _____

4. These giant stone sculptures are a grand and impressive sight. _____

5. The four presidents look out over the land from the peak of the mountain. _____

6. It was the person who carved the sculptures, Gutzon Borglum, who first saw Mount Rushmore in 1924.

   _____

7. Borglum first observed the huge mountain and knew that this was the place for his sculptures. _____

8. Calvin Coolidge, president when the first cutting of the rock began, had hoped to have a carved message that could be read from three miles away. _____

9. Coolidge gave an exciting speech before Borglum drilled the first holes in the stone. _____

10. Many workers helped in the task of creating the massive stone sculptures over a period of fourteen years. _____

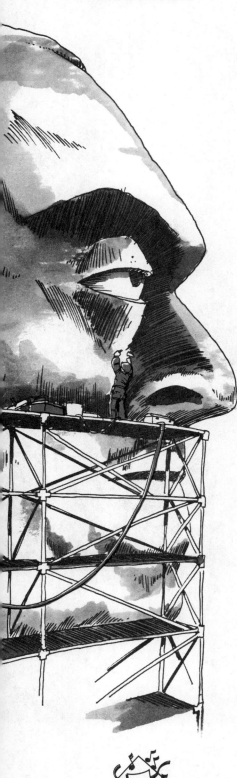

WORD GROUPS

Read each pair of words. Think about how they are alike. Write the word from the box that best completes each group.

beheld	assisted	renowned	summit
dramatic	majestic	bust	

1. top, peak, _____

2. famous, well-known, _____

3. observed, viewed, _____

4. splendid, grand, _____

5. aided, helped, _____

6. exciting, theatrical, _____

7. sculpture, figure, _____

ANALOGIES

An **analogy** compares two pairs of words. The relationship between the first pair of words is the same as the relationship between the second pair of words. Use the words in the box to complete the following analogies.

renowned	bust	sculptor
inscription	summit	carvings

1. Drawings are to pictures as _____ are to sculptures.

2. Record is to song as _____ is to writing.

3. Violinist is to violin as _____ is to sculpture.

4. Statue is to whole as _____ is to part.

5. Floor is to bottom as _____ is to top.

6. Popular is to well-liked as _____ is to famous.

CROSSWORD PUZZLE

Use the clues and the words in the box to complete the crossword puzzle.

beheld	sculptor	carvings	assisted	inscription
bust	summit	majestic	dramatic	renowned

Across
2. looked at
3. stately, grand
6. person who carves sculptures
7. carved message
9. theatrical, exciting

Down
1. well-known
2. sculpture showing the head and shoulders
4. sculptures
5. gave aid to
8. highest point of a mountain

GET WISE TO TESTS

Directions: Read each sentence carefully. Then choose the best answer to complete each sentence. Mark the space for the answer you have chosen.

 Think about the meaning of the boldfaced word. Don't be fooled by a word that looks similar to the boldfaced word.

1. **Carvings** are _____.
   Ⓐ toys
   Ⓒ sculptures
   Ⓑ cards
   Ⓓ paintings

2. The **bust** of a sculpture includes the _____.
   Ⓕ full body
   Ⓗ feet and legs
   Ⓖ rust
   Ⓙ head and shoulders

3. The **summit** of Mount Rushmore is its _____.
   Ⓐ bottom
   Ⓒ summer
   Ⓑ peak
   Ⓓ slope

4. A **sculptor** is a _____.
   Ⓕ carver
   Ⓗ catcher
   Ⓖ singer
   Ⓙ president

5. People who are **renowned** are _____.
   Ⓐ unknown
   Ⓒ famous
   Ⓑ nasty
   Ⓓ restless

6. Something **majestic** is _____.
   Ⓕ impressive
   Ⓗ many-sided
   Ⓖ Small
   Ⓙ lasting

7. When I **beheld** the mountain, I _____ it.
   Ⓐ believed
   Ⓒ carved
   Ⓑ observed
   Ⓓ bought

8. A **dramatic** speech is _____.
   Ⓕ ridiculous
   Ⓗ exciting
   Ⓖ sad
   Ⓙ dreamy

9. An **inscription** is a _____.
   Ⓐ drug store
   Ⓒ description
   Ⓑ pill
   Ⓓ carved message

10. When the workers **assisted** Borglum, they _____ him.
    Ⓕ asked
    Ⓗ hired
    Ⓖ helped
    Ⓙ left

Review

1. Something **fundamental** is _____.
   Ⓐ basic
   Ⓒ light
   Ⓑ metal
   Ⓓ fearless

2. A worker who is **fatigued** is _____.
   Ⓕ confused
   Ⓗ happy
   Ⓖ tired
   Ⓙ equal

3. Someone with **vitality** has _____.
   Ⓐ intelligence
   Ⓒ energy
   Ⓑ variety
   Ⓓ wealth

4. **Dedication** to a cause is _____.
   Ⓕ science
   Ⓗ perfection
   Ⓖ writing
   Ⓙ devotion

Writing

People who have seen Mount Rushmore are struck by the size and grandness of the sculptures. With just a few well-chosen words, you can create a poem about it. Look at the picture of Mount Rushmore. What words come to your mind? How does it make you feel?

Write a poem that expresses your thoughts and feelings. Follow the directions for each line of the poem. You can also get some ideas from the example poem below. Use some vocabulary words in your writing.

The subject (noun) ⟶	Mount Rushmore
Two adjectives ⟶	sculptured, stately
Three verbs ⟶	watching, listening, protecting
Four words naming feelings ⟶	pride, excitement, admiration, wonder
One or two words to replace the subject in the first line ⟶	stone faces

Subject: _____

Adjectives: _____

Verbs: _____

Feelings: _____

Replace the subject: _____

Turn to "My Personal Word List" on page 132. Write some words from the story or other words that you would like to know more about. Use a dictionary to find the meanings.

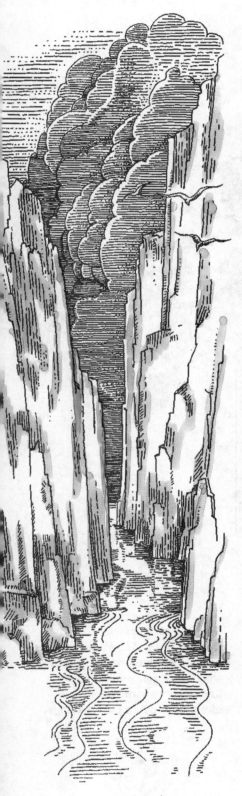

★ Read the story below. Think about the meanings of the **boldfaced** words. ★

The White Cliffs of Dover

Captain "Stormy" Stormalong and his crew have had exciting adventures while sailing aboard the ship named Tuscarora. Now they find themselves in a very troublesome situation. Their boat is stuck between the Cliffs of Dover in England! Their strange experience provides a humorous explanation of how these cliffs became white.

The crew felt that there had been enough excitement for one voyage. But the *Tuscarora's* troubles were not over. The fresh breeze died suddenly. A fog blanketed the ocean. At last the fog cleared. The *Tuscarora* had indeed worked herself into a tight spot. She had been swept into the narrow end of the North Sea, between England and Holland. As luck would have it, she was heading southwest by west. Directly ahead of her **loomed** the Straits of Dover.

At their narrowest, between Folkestone and Calais, the Straits measure about twenty miles wide. There was obviously no room in which the ship could be turned around in order to leave the North Sea through the open waters north of Scotland. The **prevailing** wind was north-northeast. Any effort to back the ship into a wider channel would be unsuccessful. Stormalong called a conference of all his officers.

The meeting in the Captain's cabin was short. When the men **emerged**, Stormy gave an order to drop anchor and put the lifeboats over the port side. The officers retired to their cabins, and quickly returned to the deck in their best dress uniforms. Five thousand barrels of pickled herrings were lowered into the lifeboats along with the officers. The little fleet headed for The Hague on the Dutch shore. As everyone knows, the Dutch are among the cleanest and tidiest people on Earth. In order to keep their houses shining and their faces glistening, they need soap — and plenty of it! They are also very fond of pickled herring.

Stormalong's officers went straight to the town hall and explained their **predicament** to the city fathers. The good Dutch burghers listened sympathetically. They were, for the most part, merchants and seafaring men themselves. They had long known and admired the reputation of Captain Stormalong and were happy to help him in his hour of need. At first they refused the gift of pickled herring. But they were finally persuaded to accept it.

Couriers were sent to every **nook** and corner of Holland, and to a few selected border towns in Belgium. Everywhere housewives opened their cupboards and gave up their stores of soap. Delicately perfumed face soap, harsh scrubbing soap, laundry soap, shaving soap, and even scouring powder, were loaded into dogcarts and trundled to the boats waiting in the harbor of The Hague. The coast of Holland was jammed with sightseers, who came with their families and picnic baskets to watch the operation.

Once the soap had been taken aboard the *Tuscarora,* Stormy put the men to work. The crew were let down over the sides in bosun's chairs, each man with a brush and a bucket of soap jelly. They spread the soap as thick as they could over the hull. At the end of a long day's work, the *Tuscarora* was smeared from stem to stern with a slippery coating. Little froths of suds, like a lace edging, encircled her water-line.

When the work was completed, Stormalong ordered the anchor hauled up, the canvas **unfurled**. Taking advantage of a brisk wind, he urged the ship forward into the narrow straits. It was a tight squeeze! The picnicking Dutchmen on the shore joined the crew in a loud cheer as the *Tuscarora* slipped through the narrow bottle-neck and cleared her way into the English Channel out onto the broad Atlantic.

The choppy waters of the Channel washed a good bit of the soap off the ship's sides. For weeks **thereafter** clouds of iridescent soap bubbles rose into the sky like round rainbows whenever the wind freshened. Bubbles are **temporary** things at best, however, and in time these were forgotten.

One permanent **souvenir** of the incident remained. As the *Tuscarora* squeezed through the narrowest channel, her **starboard** rail brushed against the cliffs on the British coast. The soap on that side was scraped off by the jutting rocks. To this day it remains there. It stands out white and clear, and has become a famous landmark for tourists. The headlands, which had before been a sandy red, were now the color of chalk. They have been known since as the White Cliffs of Dover.

From "Stormalong Fights the Kraken," in Mister Stormalong, by Anne Malcolmson and Dell J. McCormick

★ Go back to the story. Underline any words or sentences that give you clues to the meanings of the **boldfaced** words. ★

USING CONTEXT

Meanings for the vocabulary words are given below. Go back to the story and read each sentence that contains a vocabulary word. If you still cannot tell the meaning, look for clues in the sentences that come before and after the one with the vocabulary word. Write each word in front of its meaning.

predicament	souvenir	emerged	loomed
thereafter	unfurled	prevailing	nook
starboard	temporary		

1. _____: came out or came forth, especially so as to be seen

2. _____: the right side of the ship when you are facing forward

3. _____: a sheltered place; a corner

4. _____: something that you keep as a reminder of an event or place; remembrance

5. _____: to have spread out or opened; unrolled or unfolded

6. _____: after a specific time or event

7. _____: appeared in an impressive or overwhelming form

8. _____: having force, power, or influence; controlling

9. _____: a situation that is difficult, embarrassing, or dangerous

10. _____: lasting for a short or limited time; not permanent

CHALLENGE YOURSELF

Name two places from which you might take home a <u>souvenir</u>.

_____   _____

Name two things that are <u>temporary</u>.

_____   _____

SYNONYMS AND ANTONYMS

Synonyms are words that have the same or nearly the same meaning. **Antonyms** are words with opposite meanings.

Each word in the box is either a synonym or an antonym of one of the words listed below. Match each word with its synonym or antonym.

loomed	temporary	thereafter
nook	unfurled	prevailing

1. controlling _____

2. permanent _____

3. rolled _____

4. corner _____

5. appeared _____

6. later _____

REWRITING SENTENCES

Rewrite each sentence using one of the words from the box.

starboard	predicament	emerge	souvenir

1. When our friends dropped by for dinner, we were faced with an embarrassing situation because we did not have enough food.

   _____

2. I brought back an object that will help me remember the circus.

   _____

3. The captain announced that we would be able to see the famous seaport by moving to the right side of the ship.

   _____

4. On our nature hike, we observed a rabbit come forth from its hole in the ground.

   _____

GET WISE TO TESTS

Directions: Choose the word or words that best take the place of the boldfaced word. Mark your answer.

Tip This test will show how well you understand the meaning of the words. Think about the meaning of the boldfaced word before you choose your answer.

1. The **prevailing** winds made the trip longer. They were not blowing in the direction we wanted to go.
   - Ⓐ weak
   - Ⓒ controlling
   - Ⓑ available
   - Ⓓ demanding

2. The woodchuck **emerged** from its hole. But when it saw us, it ran back in.
   - Ⓕ came forth
   - Ⓗ hid in
   - Ⓖ came under
   - Ⓙ covered

3. This is some **predicament** we are in. You are ill, and I can't find a doctor!
   - Ⓐ difficult situation
   - Ⓒ hotel
   - Ⓑ funny situation
   - Ⓓ moment

4. Eating pizza every day during our vacation was too much for me. I never ate it **thereafter**.
   - Ⓕ after that time
   - Ⓗ during that time
   - Ⓖ before that time
   - Ⓙ in the past

5. The mountains **loomed** in the distance. They were more majestic than I imagined they would be.
   - Ⓐ disappeared
   - Ⓒ were forgotten
   - Ⓑ came into view
   - Ⓓ appeared hidden

6. We searched the whole house, including every **nook** and cranny. But the key was not to be found.
   - Ⓕ kitchen
   - Ⓗ shingle
   - Ⓖ cellar
   - Ⓙ corner

7. We cherish this **souvenir**. It is a reminder of a great vacation.
   - Ⓐ trip
   - Ⓒ remembrance
   - Ⓑ cruise
   - Ⓓ reservation

8. That enemy plane is off the **starboard** side. Well have to turn the ship to escape it.
   - Ⓕ left
   - Ⓗ weak
   - Ⓖ port
   - Ⓙ right

9. This pass is **temporary**. I will get another one in a few weeks.
   - Ⓐ useless
   - Ⓒ not permanent
   - Ⓑ worthless
   - Ⓓ not signed

10. We watched in silence as the flag **unfurled** in the breeze. We always raise it on the Fourth of July.
    - Ⓕ opened
    - Ⓗ dropped
    - Ⓖ closed
    - Ⓙ whipped

Review

1. She is a **renowned** artist. Everyone knows her work.
   - Ⓐ unknown
   - Ⓒ flashy
   - Ⓑ famous
   - Ⓓ reckless

2. We have a **bust** of George Washington in our school. It is made of stone.
   - Ⓕ horse
   - Ⓗ relic
   - Ⓖ full figure
   - Ⓙ head and shoulders

Writing

Captain Stormalong and his sailors faced quite a predicament. So they went to others to ask for help. Think about a time when you or someone you know faced a predicament. What was done to resolve the situation?

Write a paragraph that tells about the experience. Explain what the predicament was. Then describe the solution that was found. Use some vocabulary words in your writing.

_Today I faced
a real predicame_

_____

_____

_____

_____

_____

_____

_____

_____

_____

_____

_____

_____

_____

_____

_____

_____

_____

Turn to "My Personal Word List" on page 132. Write some words from the story or other words that you would like to know more about. Use a dictionary to find the meanings.

★ Read the story below. Think about the meanings of the **boldfaced** words. ★

Resting Place for a King

When a person dies today, **burial** is usually in the ground, in a cemetery. The grave is marked with a single stone. When an Egyptian **pharaoh** died thousands of years ago, his grave was also marked with stone. But this king's grave was in the form of a huge stone pyramid. This mighty structure housed the dead body. The body was wrapped in layers of cloth. Then the **mummy** was placed in a secret room in the pyramid.

The amazing thing about these tombs is that they were built without machines or modern tools. Workers cut giant blocks of stone from nearby quarries. Holes were cut in the stone and wedges of wood placed in the holes. The stone was then soaked in water. The wooden wedges absorbed the water, expanded, and broke the stone into smaller blocks. Each block weighed over a ton.

Using ropes, huge gangs of men then dragged the blocks to the construction area. The first layer of stone was pushed into position. Other blocks were **elevated** to the next higher level using earthen ramps. The **incline** of the ramps was made steeper to raise the blocks to the upper levels. Finally, the whole pyramid was covered with white stone.

Who built the pyramids? Students of **archaeology**, the science that studies objects from the past, believe it was farmers. They worked on the pyramids during the months when the Nile River flooded the farmers' lands. At that rate, this **tedious** work may have taken 100,000 men as long as 50 years to finish just one pyramid.

The **triangular** shape of the pyramid walls is thought to have had **spiritual** meaning for the Egyptians. They believed this three-sided shape would help the pharaoh reach heaven. Archaeologists think that the Egyptians designed the pyramid's **diagonal** sides to imitate the sun's slanting rays. The pharaoh's soul could climb the shining rays to join the gods.

★ Go back to the story. Underline the words or sentences that give you a clue to the meaning of each **boldfaced** word. ★

CONTEXT CLUES

Read each sentence. Look for clues to help you complete each
sentence with a word from the box. Write the word on the line.

pharaoh	burial	archaeology	incline
mummy	elevated	triangular	spiritual
tedious	diagonal		

1. The method of _____ for many people who
   have died is to place them in a grave marked with a stone.

2. The grave of an Egyptian king, or _____, was
   marked by a pyramid built with stones.

3. The pharaoh's body was wrapped in layers of cloth, and the

   _____ was placed in a secret room inside
   the pyramid.

4. The Egyptian pyramids are amazing structures because the huge

   stone blocks were raised, or _____, on ramps
   without the use of machines.

5. Imagine how steep the _____ of the ramps had
   to be to raise the stones to such great heights.

6. Students of _____, who study objects of the
   past, believe it was farmers who built the pyramids.

7. Some historians say 50 years was not an unusual amount of time
   spent to build the huge pyramids with three-sided, or

   _____, sides.

8. Most workers spent their lives and their strength doing the

   _____ job of building the pyramids.

9. The pyramids' _____ sides, which slant
   downward, may have been designed to imitate the sun's
   slanting rays.

10. It is thought that the triangular shape of the pyramids' sides had

    _____ meaning for the Egyptians in that the
    shape would somehow help the pharaoh reach heaven.

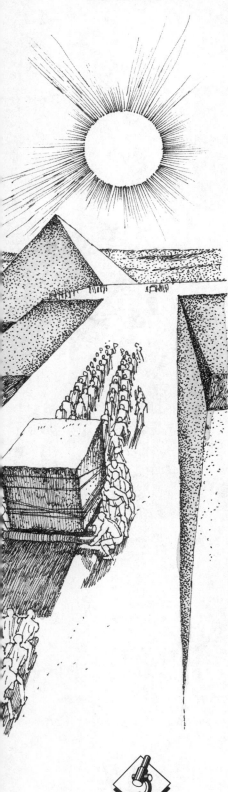

WORD SENSE

Read each phrase. Check the Dictionary to see if the words make sense together. If they do, write yes on the line. If they do not, write a new word that does make sense with the underlined word.

1. tedious work _____

2. triangular pencil _____

3. Roman pharaoh _____

4. diagonal sides _____

5. burial room _____

6. fat incline _____

7. songs of archaeology _____

8. blocks elevated _____

9. mummy talked _____

10. spiritual ramp _____

MULTIPLE MEANINGS

The words in the box have more than one meaning. Look for clues in each sentence to tell which meaning is being used. Write the letter of the meaning next to the correct sentence.

incline	spiritual
a. a sloping surface	**a.** relating to the spirit or soul
b. to bend or bow	**b.** a religious song
elevated	
a. raised or lifted up	
b. improved the mind or emotions	

_____ 1. The people incline their heads to the king.

_____ 2. The car got stuck going up the icy incline.

_____ 3. Everyone joined together to sing the spiritual.

_____ 4. Some people believe that shapes of things have spiritual meanings.

_____ 5. The stone blocks were elevated by ropes.

_____ 6. The speech elevated the audience's mood.

GET WISE TO TESTS

Directions: Read each sentence. Pick the word that best completes the sentence. Mark the answer space for that word.

 Tip Some tests put letters before the answer choices. Be sure to find the letter of the answer you think is correct, then fill in the circle beside it.

1. Of all Egyptian kings, Tut is the most famous _____.
Ⓐ burial
Ⓑ burying
Ⓒ pharaoh
Ⓓ royalty

2. Tut's _____ is wrapped tightly in cloth.
Ⓕ pharaoh
Ⓖ shining
Ⓗ mummy
Ⓙ carefully

3. The study of ancient times is called _____.
Ⓐ archaeology
Ⓑ scientific
Ⓒ ancient
Ⓓ mostly

4. The ___ place of King Tut is visited by many people.
Ⓕ bury
Ⓖ burial
Ⓗ archaeology
Ⓙ their

5. All pyramid walls have a _____, or three-sided shape.
Ⓐ rounding
Ⓑ diagonal
Ⓒ triangular
Ⓓ pharaoh

6. The _____ of the ramp must have been very steep.
Ⓕ elevator
Ⓖ triangular
Ⓗ motioned
Ⓙ incline

7. It took many men to get the stones _____.
Ⓐ tedious
Ⓑ elevated
Ⓒ chopped
Ⓓ diagonal

8. Working on the pyramids was a _____ job.
Ⓕ pharaoh
Ⓖ captured
Ⓗ greatly
Ⓙ tedious

9. The shape of the pyramids had _____ meaning.
Ⓐ returned
Ⓑ overly
Ⓒ spiritual
Ⓓ incline

10. The _____ sides of the pyramids may have imitated the sun's rays.
Ⓕ royal
Ⓖ forever
Ⓗ almost
Ⓙ diagonal

Review

1. The large statue stood in a _____ in the hall.
Ⓐ jar
Ⓑ nook
Ⓒ painting
Ⓓ double

2. The groundhog _____ from its hole and saw its shadow.
Ⓕ emerged
Ⓖ entered
Ⓗ happy
Ⓙ slowly

3. I bought a postcard as a _____ of the trip.
Ⓐ letter
Ⓑ scenery
Ⓒ beautiful
Ⓓ souvenir

4. We rushed to the _____ side of the ship to look at the whales.
Ⓕ starboard
Ⓖ floating
Ⓗ admire
Ⓙ mixture

SCIENCE
WORLD WONDERS
LESSON 15

Writing

Pretend that you are an archaeologist living in the year 3089. You are studying buildings, objects, and other things left from our present civilization. What do you think of the buildings and objects? What ideas do you get about the people from looking at these artifacts?

Write a paragraph expressing your views. Think about what the buildings and objects reveal about the people. Use some vocabulary words in your writing.

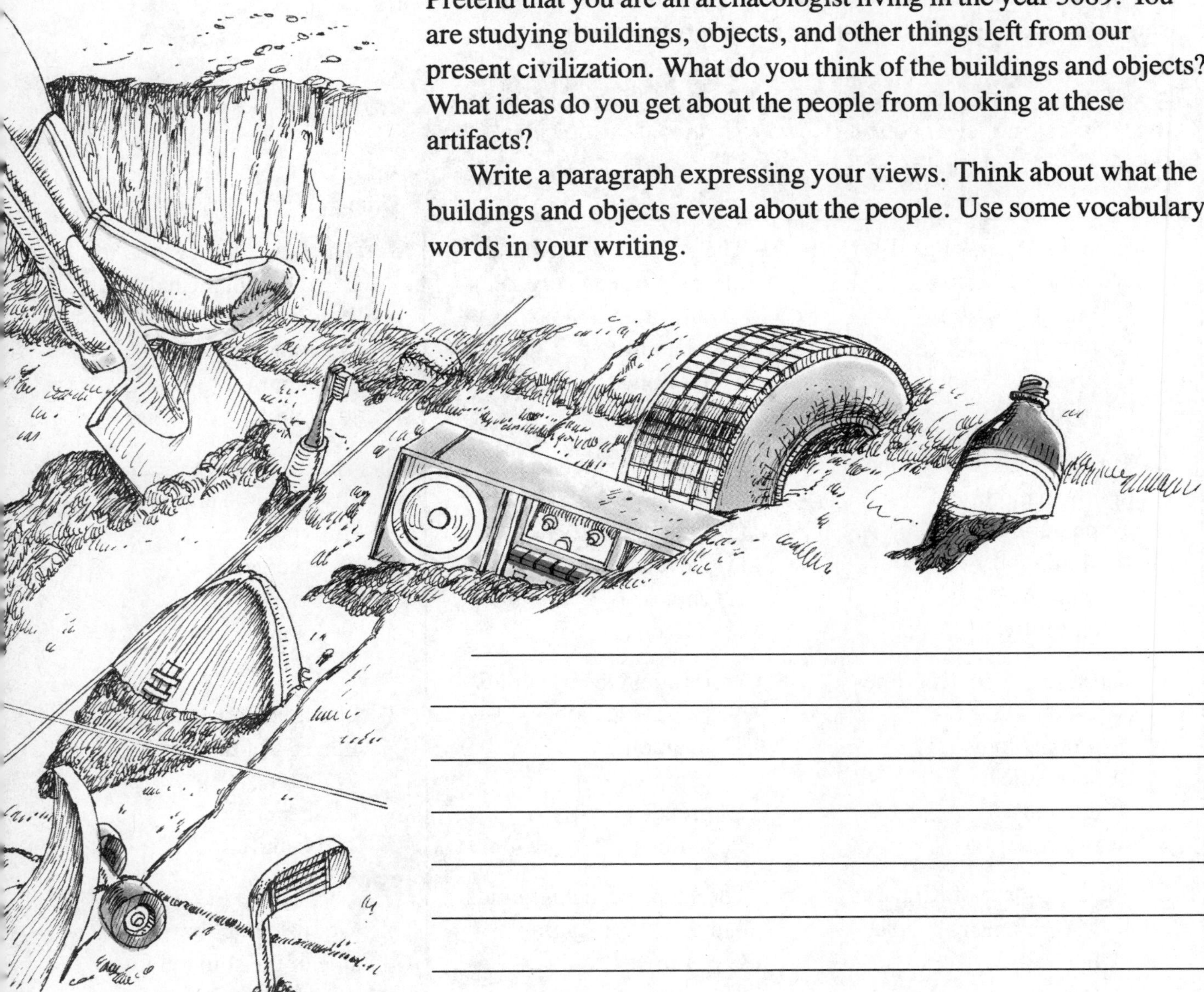

Turn to "My Personal Word List" on page 132. Write some words from the story or other words that you would like to know more about. Use a dictionary to find the meanings.

★ Read the story below. Think about the meanings of the **boldfaced** words. ★

Wall of Wonder

Have you ever thought about the walls of your house as your own personal means of protection? They are. They protect you from the weather outside. More important, they let you decide which people you want to come inside. Two thousand years ago, the Chinese had the same idea. But they built a wall around their entire country!

The Great Wall of China was built at the command of China's first emperor. Before his reign, China was split into several warring states, each surrounded by its own wall. The emperor united these states. One way of showing their **unity** was to have one wall surrounding all of China.

The emperor claimed that the wall's purpose was **defensive**. It was intended to protect China from attacks by the fierce **nomads** who wandered the Gobi Desert, north of China. Also, it displayed the emperor's power. He forced a million men to work on the wall. Many of them had been his enemies. For most, becoming a **laborer** was a death sentence. So many men died in building the Great Wall that it has been called "the longest cemetery in the world."

Later emperors built **extensions** onto the Great Wall to make it longer. Today it measures 3,700 miles along China's northern border. But the wall never really protected the empire from **conquest**. The wandering warriors of the north swept across it numerous times to take over the country. Perhaps it was not as a physical barrier, but as an idea, that the wall protected China. The Chinese came to think of everyone "inside the wall" as belonging together.

The Great Wall has **withstood** over two thousand years of harsh weather and invading armies. This **architectural** marvel winds like a snake across varied **terrains**, which include mountains, valleys, and rivers. It is one of the world's most **awesome** wonders.

★ Go back to the story. Underline the words or sentences that give you a clue to the meaning of each **boldfaced** word. ★

CONTEXT CLUES

In each sentence a word or phrase is underlined. Choose a word from the box to replace that word or phrase. Write the word on the line.

nomads	withstood	laborer	extensions
unity	defensive	awesome	architectural
terrains	conquest		

1. The Great Wall of China has underlined endured bad weather and invading armies. _____

2. China's first emperor ordered that the wall be built for protective measures. _____

3. Fierce wanderers of the Gobi Desert were at times stopped from attacking by the huge wall, but, in the end, they did sweep across it. _____

4. The Great Wall of China did provide the people with a feeling of belonging together, of being a whole country instead of a group of warring states. _____

5. But for anyone who was a worker on the wall, it was a death sentence. _____

6. The varied areas of land upon which the wall was built made work very difficult. _____

7. Not only did many men die working on the original wall, but thousands more died building added parts ordered by later emperors. _____

8. No matter how many extensions were added, the wall did not prevent a victory over China at the hands of the wandering warriors. _____

9. Although China has changed greatly, the building design of the Wall has barely changed. _____

10. The Great Wall of China is one of the most magnificent wonders of the world. _____

CLOZE PARAGRAPH

Use the words in the box to complete the passage. Then reread the passage to be sure it makes sense.

withstood	terrains	nomads	extensions
laborer	defensive	unity	architectural
awesome	conquest		

To build the Great Wall, people needed to work together

in (1) _____. Every (2) _____
who worked on the wall was skilled, and many different materials
were used. As a result, the Great Wall has endured thousands of

years of bad weather as well as (3) _____ the

attacks of invading armies. Its (4) _____ design is
so solid that it will most likely last forever.

Over the years, new parts, (5) _____,
lengthened the Great Wall. Still, it did not always serve as a

(6) _____ structure against attackers. The

(7) _____ that wandered the desert were
determined to win control of China. In spite of the wall, they
sometimes gained control of the land through military

(8) _____.

Today, tourists from all over the world travel to see the Great
Wall. A traveler in a plane could see it snake and loop for some
3,700 miles across valleys, mountains, and other

(9) _____. It is an (10) _____
sight, filling all who see it with wonder.

WORD MAP

Words can be put on a kind of map to show what they have in common. Use the vocabulary words in the box to complete the word map about the Great Wall of China. Add another word you know to each group.

withstood	nomads	defensive	laborers	extensions
terrains	unity	conquest	awesome	architectural

Why Built

_____ of country

_____ measures

_____

_____

How Built

millions of _____

across many _____

several _____

_____

GREAT WALL OF CHINA

After the Wall Was Built

_____ attacked

military _____

_____ weather

Words That Describe It

_____ wonder

_____ marvel

_____

98

GET WISE TO TESTS

Directions: Read the phrase. Look for the word or words that have the same or almost the same meaning as the boldfaced word. Mark the answer space for your choice.

Tip Always read all the answer choices. Many choices may make sense. But only one answer choice has the same or almost the same meaning as the boldfaced word.

1. tired **laborer**
   - Ⓐ nomad
   - Ⓑ warrior
   - Ⓒ worker
   - Ⓓ rider

2. **architectural** design
   - Ⓕ defensive
   - Ⓖ building
   - Ⓗ popular
   - Ⓙ awesome

3. wall **extensions**
   - Ⓐ rocky terrains
   - Ⓑ added parts
   - Ⓒ long strings
   - Ⓓ long directions

4. **defensive** measures
   - Ⓕ simple
   - Ⓖ awesome
   - Ⓗ dull
   - Ⓙ protective

5. rough **terrains**
   - Ⓐ areas of land
   - Ⓑ thunderstorms
   - Ⓒ stores
   - Ⓓ materials

6. feeling of **unity**
   - Ⓕ confusion
   - Ⓖ victory
   - Ⓗ sadness
   - Ⓙ togetherness

7. **withstood** attacks
   - Ⓐ lost
   - Ⓑ endured
   - Ⓒ ignored
   - Ⓓ understood

8. army's **conquest**
   - Ⓕ defense
   - Ⓖ victory
   - Ⓗ uniform
   - Ⓙ unity

9. **awesome** sight
   - Ⓐ huge
   - Ⓑ forgotten
   - Ⓒ usual
   - Ⓓ magnificent

10. fierce **nomads**
    - Ⓕ dogs
    - Ⓖ wanderers
    - Ⓗ emperors
    - Ⓙ walls

Review

1. Egyptian **pharaoh**
   - Ⓐ farmer
   - Ⓑ laborer
   - Ⓒ king
   - Ⓓ phone

2. **supreme** achievement
   - Ⓕ silly
   - Ⓖ highest
   - Ⓗ careful
   - Ⓙ certain

3. **triangular** shape
   - Ⓐ odd
   - Ⓑ regular
   - Ⓒ ten-sided
   - Ⓓ three-sided

4. two-hour **session**
   - Ⓕ sale
   - Ⓖ practice time
   - Ⓗ show time
   - Ⓙ battle

5. **fundamental** skills
   - Ⓐ funny
   - Ⓑ basic
   - Ⓒ tricky
   - Ⓓ proven

Writing

The Great Wall of China has been a popular tourist sight for many years. One section most often visited by tourists is the Badling Pass. Another is the Shanhaiguan Gate, on the far eastern section of the wall.

Imagine that you have been hired to create an advertisement to persuade more people to visit the Great Wall. Use facts from the story and the scene on this page to help you stir up excitement about the wall. Be sure to use colorful words to persuade people to plan a trip. Use some vocabulary words in your writing.

Make history come alive for you.
Visit the Great Wall of China!

Turn to "My Personal Word List" on page 132. Write some words from the story or other words that you would like to know more about. Use a dictionary to find the meanings.

_____

_____

_____

_____

_____

_____

_____

_____

★ To review the words in Lessons 13–16, turn to page 128. ★

GLITTERING GOLD

Gold has been used for money and jewelry throughout history. It is as valuable as it is beautiful.

In Lessons 17–20, you will read about how people find gold. You'll also read about a place with a twenty-ton door where a large amount of this precious metal is stored. Name some objects that are made from gold. Think of some words that can describe this dazzling metal. Write your ideas under the headings below.

Objects Made From Gold   **Words That Describe Gold**

_____   _____

_____   _____

_____   _____

_____   _____

_____   _____

★ Read the story below. Think about the meanings of the **boldfaced** words. ★

Gold!

January 24, 1848, was just another workday for carpenter James Marshall. He was building a sawmill for John Sutter. Sutter owned a portion of land on the American River in California. Bending down, Marshall saw something glitter in the water. To his surprise, it was several nuggets of gold.

Word of the discovery of gold spread quickly. Gold fever was like an **epidemic**. But it was not a spreading sickness. From near and far, hopeful people rushed to California in **anticipation** of striking it rich. On February 28, 1849, the first shipful of gold seekers arrived in San Francisco. They, and the thousands who followed them, were called "forty-niners."

The **craze** for gold drove people in the East to give up good jobs and rush westward to find their fortune. Once they arrived, the miners used a pan or a sifter called a cradle to find nuggets in streams or rivers. They rocked water and gravel back and forth in the cradle. This sifted out the lighter sand and left any gold in the bottom. Some traced the gold to its source in the mountains and used **dynamite** to blow it out.

Many miners lived in **shanties**, run-down shacks built quickly and crudely. Their lives were **solitary** and often lonely. Miners **distrusted** one another, so they seldom worked together. They were afraid that someone would cheat them out of the gold they had worked so hard to find.

Those who did strike it rich often rushed to town to spend their money freely. Many more miners, however, found no gold and returned home **empty-handed**. Some gave up because of **homesickness** and went back to the places they had left. But many people who did not find gold stayed in California anyway. They settled on **homesteads**, where they raised cattle or farmed. When the California Gold Rush ended, it left behind few millionaires. But it had produced a young and growing state.

★ Go back to the story. Underline the words or sentences that give you a clue to the meaning of each **boldfaced** word. ★

CONTEXT CLUES

In each sentence a word or phrase is underlined. Choose a word from the box to replace that word or phrase. Write the word on the line.

anticipation	epidemic	empty-handed	dynamite
homesickness	shanties	distrusted	craze
homesteads	solitary		

1. News of the discovery of gold was like a rapidly spreading outbreak of the measles. _____

2. In 1849, over 80,000 people headed west to find gold in California with eager expectation. _____

3. The popular, short-lived madness for gold became known as the gold rush. _____

4. Some miners used an explosive to blow up the mountains and get at the rock that contained the gold. _____

5. When not digging or blowing up mountains, miners lived in run-down shacks made of wood. _____

6. A gold miner led a lonely and private life, keeping away from other miners. _____

7. The miners did not trust each other and were afraid of being cheated or robbed. _____

8. After months and even years of work, many miners found no gold and went home having gained nothing.

   _____

9. One reason that many miners gave up the search for gold was a longing for home and family. _____

10. Though few struck it rich, many were given land to farm, improve, and eventually own. _____

WORD ORIGINS

Knowing the origin of a word can help you understand its meaning. Read each word origin. Then write each word from the box next to its origin.

homestead	epidemic	dynamite
solitary	distrust	anticipation

1. from Latin <u>solus</u>, alone _____

2. from Greek <u>dynamikos</u>, powerful _____

3. from Old English <u>hāmstede</u>, property _____

4. from Greek <u>epi</u>, among + <u>demos</u>, people _____

5. from Latin <u>anticipāt(us)</u> + <u>ion</u>, taken before _____

6. from <u>dis</u>, not + German <u>trost</u>, comfort _____

CLOZE PARAGRAPH

Use the words in the box to complete the paragraph. Then reread it to be sure it makes sense.

distrusted	empty-handed	anticipation	solitary
craze	homesickness	shanties	

The (1) _____ for gold brought so many families into California that in 1850 it became a state. This started other gold rushes. In 1859, in (2) _____ of striking it rich, people moved to Colorado with the Pike's Peak gold rush. The gold seekers appeared and built (3) _____.

The miners lived their (4) _____ lives and faced

(5) _____. The miners at Pike's Peak

(6) _____ other miners, too. And just as before, some found riches. Others left (7) _____.

WORD RIDDLE

Write each word from the box next to its definition. Then write the boxed letters in order in the blanks below. You will find the answer to this riddle.

What did the miner call his barely furnished shack?

epidemic	shanties	empty-handed	craze
anticipation	distrusted	homesteads	dynamite
homesickness	solitary		

1. a popular, short-lived madness __ __ ☐ __ __

2. lacked trust or confidence in __ __ __ __ __ __ ☐ __ __

3. sudden spread of an idea or disease __ __ __ __ __ __ __ ☐

4. the act of expecting __ __ __ __ __ __ __ ☐ __ __ __

5. blasting explosive __ __ ☐ __ __ __ __ __

6. being away from people; alone __ __ __ __ ☐ __ __ ☐

7. condition of missing one's home and family __ __ __ __ ☐ __ __ __ __ __ __ __

8. land given to people to work and improve ☐ __ __ __ __ __ __ ☐ __ __ __

9. broken-down shacks __ __ __ ☐ __ __ __ __

10. having nothing __ __ __ ☐☐ __ __ __ __ __ __

ANSWER:

__ __ __ __ __ __ __ __ __ __ __ __ __ __ __!

GET WISE TO TESTS

Directions: Read the sentences. Look for the best word to use in the blank. Mark the answer space for your choice.

 Before you choose an answer, try reading the sentences with each answer choice. This will help you choose an answer that makes sense.

1. Everyone has gold rush fever. The _____ is spreading.
   - Ⓐ medicine
   - Ⓑ dynamite
   - Ⓒ epidemic
   - Ⓓ gold

2. I would not like to live alone. I don't care for a _____ life.
   - Ⓕ long
   - Ⓖ solitary
   - Ⓗ hungry
   - Ⓙ supreme

3. The store was out of everything. We went home _____.
   - Ⓐ satisfied
   - Ⓑ solitary
   - Ⓒ empty-handed
   - Ⓓ underwater

4. The miners blasted the mountains with explosives. They used _____.
   - Ⓕ homesteads
   - Ⓖ tools
   - Ⓗ horses
   - Ⓙ dynamite

5. People dreamed about gold. They were willing to risk everything in _____ of striking it rich.
   - Ⓐ anticipation
   - Ⓑ destruction
   - Ⓒ dynamite
   - Ⓓ fear

6. He kept everything to himself. He _____ everyone.
   - Ⓕ married
   - Ⓖ distrusted
   - Ⓗ paid
   - Ⓙ trusted

7. She missed her family. She had a case of _____.
   - Ⓐ homesickness
   - Ⓑ homesteads
   - Ⓒ books
   - Ⓓ dynamite

8. Look at the broken-down shacks. Those _____ are deserted.
   - Ⓕ homesteads
   - Ⓖ shanties
   - Ⓗ prices
   - Ⓙ boards

9. People were given land to farm. They lived on _____.
   - Ⓐ mountains
   - Ⓑ homesickness
   - Ⓒ livestock
   - Ⓓ homesteads

10. What will be the next popular, short-lived madness? No one can predict the next _____.
   - Ⓕ story
   - Ⓖ epidemic
   - Ⓗ craze
   - Ⓙ condition

Review

1. The corn is high this year. The farm _____ is proud of his work.
   - Ⓐ tractor
   - Ⓑ laborer
   - Ⓒ road
   - Ⓓ barn

2. The wagon train moved slowly. The rocky _____ of the west created many difficulties.
   - Ⓕ rain
   - Ⓖ sickness
   - Ⓗ terrains
   - Ⓙ deer

Writing

Imagine that you are a miner during the gold rush of 1849. You are in a mining camp, living in a shanty near the American River in California. You have been there for several months, but you have not yet found gold. How do you feel about your life there? Are your hopes for finding gold still high?

Write a letter to a friend back east describing what your life is like and how you feel about it. Also tell how you pan for gold. Use the pictures and information from the story to help you. Use some vocabulary words in your writing.

August 1849

Dear _____,

_____

_____

_____

_____

_____

_____

_____

_____

_____

_____

_____

_____

_____

Turn to "My Personal Word List" on page 132. Write some words from the story or other words that you would like to know more about. Use a dictionary to find the meanings.

★ Read the story below. Think about the meanings of the **boldfaced** words. ★

El Dorado, the City of Gold

For hundreds of years, explorers sought El Dorado, the City of Gold.

Centuries before Columbus, three great civilizations — Inca, Aztec, and Chibcha — flourished in the New World. High in the Andes Mountains of present-day Colombia in South America and some 7,500 feet above sea level, the Chibchas, specifically the Muisca tribe, ruled the **isolated** plateau of Bogotá, called Cundinamarca.

Near Cundinamarca's capital lies Lake Guatavita. Muisca legend had it that the wife of one of the kings had drowned herself there, became the "Goddess of the Lake," and now required annual placation. At some unknown point in pre-Colombian history — the Chibchas had no written records — the custom began for the ruling King to strip naked, cover himself with resinous gums, and roll in gold dust. In a canoe, followed by his subjects, he paddled to the center of the 400-foot lake, threw emeralds and gold trinkets in the water and then, "in a flash of brightness," plunged into the water to wash himself. When the Spanish heard the story, they called the King *el hombre dorado* (the **gilded** man), which was later shortened to *El Dorado* and came to mean "golden city."

Gold, of course, meant nothing to the Indians. You could neither eat it nor buy anything with it. However, in the Americas it was **abundant** and so pure that it didn't need to be refined by the mercury process used for European gold. And it was considered ornamental. Indians decorated themselves with golden nose and ear plugs and breastplates, so that they would "blaze in the sun," and used sheets of beaten gold as wind chimes outside their houses.

In Europe the Spanish Kings in the late 15th and 16th centuries were nearly bankrupt. Almost as bad, when the first shipments of gold from Mexico began arriving in the Old World, **economic** stability was thrown out of balance. Still the *conquistadores* — the Spanish **conquerors** — as well as other Europeans, were seized with gold fever. Historian Joachim Leithauser says point-blank that gold was "the object of almost every voyage of exploration."

So much gold had already been found in the New World that no one doubted that somewhere there was a whole kingdom of gold. Expeditions approached Cundinamarca by river and by jungle. The journals left behind by these gold-crazed Europeans described harrowing experiences and sufferings . . . all for El Dorado.

As late as 1595 Domingo de Vera, governor of Trinidad, persuaded the Spanish King to authorize yet another overland search for El Dorado. Sir Walter Raleigh talked his way out of imprisonment in the Tower of London with his plans for an English expedition to El Dorado to be **sponsored** by James I. This was in 1617, and when he returned to England in 1618 without the promised cargo of limitless gold, he was beheaded.

Still the myth of El Dorado **persisted**. Seventeenth-century maps continued to show it, and by then it had become "the largest citie in the entyre world." Inevitably, after nearly a century of unfulfilled **expectations**, a few disbelievers appeared.

The great Prussian scientist Alexander von Humboldt, beginning in 1799, scientifically and with Germanic thoroughness retraced all the steps taken by earlier seekers of El Dorado.

Humboldt made some computations: If every year for a century 1,000 Indians dropped five trinkets of gold in the lake, there would be 500,000 gold pieces.

Humboldt, despite his lofty intentions of dispelling the myth, started a worldwide rage for draining the lake. The most exhaustive attempt was made in 1912 by Contractors, Ltd., of London. They shipped $150,000 worth of equipment to Colombia and lowered the level of the lake, already half dried up by a long drought. From the mud they reclaimed $10,000 worth of gold. But it had cost some $160,000.

El Dorado from the beginning belonged to the **category** of "lost cities" and "lands of nowhere." But too many imaginations had been captured by the **concept** of a place with streets of gold.

However, the Chibchas high in their plateau of Bogotá had at the very beginning given the first discoverers their truest gold: the potato. It was from here that the strange tuber with its vinelike leaves and purplish flower came to the Western world. With its introduction into the diet of Europeans, famine was for a time abolished from their lives — a gift more precious than any metal.

From "The Continuing Search for . . . El Dorado, the City of Gold," by Faubion Bowers from The People's ALMANAC®, by David Wallechinsky and Irving Wallace

★ Go back to the story. Underline any words or sentences that give you clues to the meanings of the **boldfaced** words. ★

CONTEXT CLUES

Read each sentence. Look for clues to help you complete each sentence with a word from the box. Write the word on the line.

abundant	economic	gilded	sponsored
persisted	conquerors	concept	category
expectations	isolated		

1. Living in the _____ area of Bogotá, the Muisca tribe was far from any other people.

2. The Spanish _____ wanted to take control of the New World tribes because many people in Europe wanted the gold that the tribes had.

3. The _____ of a place where the streets were paved with gold was an idea that drove Europeans to cross the ocean.

4. Gold was so _____, or plentiful, in the New World that the people there did not consider it valuable.

5. But in Europe, where the _____ system was suffering, more gold for trading would provide more buying power and control over money matters.

6. The rulers of several European countries _____, or paid for, explorations of Mexico in hopes of finding vast amounts of gold.

7. Although their _____ of finding riches were high, the rulers' hopes for success were dampened by what the explorers actually found.

8. In spite of the disappointments, Europeans _____, continuing firmly and steadily in hopes of becoming rich with New World gold.

9. Many Europeans remained spellbound by stories they had heard of a _____ man, who covered his body with gold.

10. The hunt for gold belongs to a _____, or group, of stories about how riches can become so important to some people.

DICTIONARY SKILLS

Read each question. For a "yes" answer, write <u>yes</u> on the line. For a "no" answer, write a sentence that gives the correct meaning of the underlined word. Use the Dictionary if you need help.

abundant	conquerors	gilded
persisted	isolated	sponsored

1. Does an <u>isolated</u> place have traffic problems?

_____

2. If you <u>persisted</u> at something, would you give it up?

_____

3. Are <u>conquerors</u> likely to try to force their will on people?

_____

4. When something is <u>gilded,</u> is it covered with armor?

_____

5. Is an <u>abundant</u> supply likely to run out soon?

_____

6. If you <u>sponsored</u> something, would you be paying for it?

_____

WORD GROUPS

Read each pair of words and think about how they are alike. Write the word from the box that completes each group.

expectations	category	economic	concept

1. idea, thought, _____

2. hopes, desires, _____

3. political, social, _____

4. class, group, _____

GET WISE TO TESTS

Directions: Read each sentence. Pick the word that best completes the sentence. Mark the answer space for that word.

 Read carefully. Use the other words in the sentence to help you choose the missing word.

Review

1. They could not find a thing in the stores and came home _____.
   Ⓐ solitary
   Ⓑ empty-headed
   Ⓒ empty-handed
   Ⓓ amazing

2. The bank robbers used _____ to blow open the safe.
   Ⓕ wind
   Ⓖ explode
   Ⓗ heat
   Ⓙ dynamite

3. He is a _____ person and never minds being alone.
   Ⓐ solitary
   Ⓑ quietly
   Ⓒ distrusted
   Ⓓ lively

4. The _____ of seeing a rock star kept the crowd hanging around the stage door for hours.
   Ⓕ craze
   Ⓖ hoping
   Ⓗ anticipation
   Ⓙ delightful

---

1. They _____ in looking until they found the gold.
   Ⓐ gilded
   Ⓑ change
   Ⓒ persisted
   Ⓓ usually

2. They had high _____ of winning the championship.
   Ⓕ expectations
   Ⓖ isolated
   Ⓗ produced
   Ⓙ foreheads

3. In that country's _____ system, fish were more valuable than gold.
   Ⓐ enter
   Ⓑ economic
   Ⓒ category
   Ⓓ further

4. They had an _____ supply of building materials.
   Ⓕ expectations
   Ⓖ eager
   Ⓗ answered
   Ⓙ abundant

5. There is a whole _____ of stories about lost cities.
   Ⓐ friendly
   Ⓑ economic
   Ⓒ establishing
   Ⓓ category

6. The _____ took over the land and made it theirs.
   Ⓕ conquerors
   Ⓖ expectations
   Ⓗ cheerfully
   Ⓙ golden

7. The house was _____ from the others by a hill.
   Ⓐ isolated
   Ⓑ operating
   Ⓒ idea
   Ⓓ abundant

8. The school _____ the show by paying all the bills.
   Ⓕ persisted
   Ⓖ outline
   Ⓗ sponsored
   Ⓙ distant

9. The edges of the pages were _____ to make the book look attractive.
   Ⓐ everybody
   Ⓑ gilded
   Ⓒ sponsored
   Ⓓ although

10. The _____ of a city of gold attracted people.
    Ⓕ economic
    Ⓖ hopeful
    Ⓗ defeated
    Ⓙ concept

Writing

The article you read says that the potato turned out to be "the truest gold" that the Europeans got from the New World. It was "a gift more precious than any metal."

Write a paragraph about something that is more precious to you than gold. It may be an object or feelings you share with others. Explain why it is so precious to you. Use some vocabulary words in your writing.

_____

_____

_____

_____

_____

_____

_____

_____

Turn to "My Personal Word List" on page 132. Write some words from the story or other words that you would like to know more about. Use a dictionary to find the meanings.

_____

_____

_____

_____

★ Read the story below. Think about the meanings of the **boldfaced** words. ★

Riches from the Earth

Today's gold mining has come a long way from the simple days of the California Gold Rush. New **technology** has replaced the pan and other crude **utensils** of more than a century ago. Now machines can do the work of hundreds of lone miners.

There have been many discoveries and **breakthroughs** in the way gold is mined. In one modern method, a machine with special buckets lifts gold-bearing dirt from river bottoms. In another, a **compressor** sends a powerful stream of water to wash sand into troughs, where any gold is trapped. Unfortunately, some of these processes destroy land and rivers. They have been stopped in many countries in the name of **conservation**.

Gold has many uses. Because it can be melted and shaped easily, gold is used to make coins for money around the world. The **richness** of gold's bright shine has made it a favorite with jewelry makers. They use gold and precious stones to **construct** beautiful jewelry.

Gold can also be hammered into thin sheets called gold leaf. People have found many **ingenious** and clever uses for this fine material. Gold leaf is used for printing on the spines of books and for decorating china and other kinds of dishes. Dentists even use gold leaf to make fillings for teeth.

Scientists have spent years doing **painstaking** research on gold's use as a medicine. Their careful work has shown that gold in liquid form can be **injected** into patients' muscles to treat several diseases. Astronomers coat telescope mirrors with a gold film because it reflects light so well. Gold has been used in space travel, too. A thin coating of gold has proved to be excellent protection for metals on the outside of satellites and other space vehicles. Of all of the earth's riches, few are as useful as gold.

★ Go back to the story. Underline the words or sentences that give you a clue to the meaning of each **boldfaced** word. ★

USING CONTEXT

Meanings for the vocabulary words are given below. Go back to the story and read each sentence that has a vocabulary word. If you still cannot tell the meaning, look for clues in the sentences that come before and after the one with the vocabulary word. Write each word in front of its meaning.

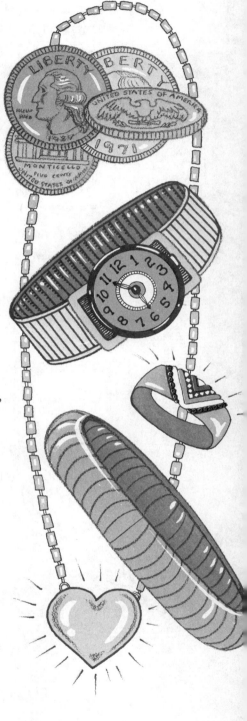

compressor	richness	ingenious	construct
breakthroughs	utensils	injected	technology
conservation	painstaking		

1. _____ : the quality of being deep, vivid, or full, as in color

2. _____ : design and make; put together

3. _____ : unusually clever and creative; showing great imagination

4. _____ : important discoveries and developments that help to improve something

5. _____ : the protecting and preserving from loss, harm, or waste, especially land, bodies of water, and wildlife

6. _____ : scientific methods and devices for doing something in a better, easier, and more practical way

7. _____ : careful, particular way of doing something

8. _____ : tools

9. _____ : machine that pushes, squeezes, or presses something into a smaller space, creating a force of power such as air or water

10. _____ : forced into, as with a needle

SYNONYMS

Synonyms are words that have the same or almost the same meaning. Write a word from the box that is a synonym of the underlined word in each sentence.

breakthroughs	ingenious	utensils	construct

1. The <u>tools</u> used today in mining gold are quite different from

   the _____ used a century ago.

2. The new technology is a result of <u>discoveries</u>,

   or _____, in ways to mine gold.

3. There are many <u>clever</u> uses for gold, such as

   the _____ use of gold to treat diseases.

4. If I had some gold, I would <u>make</u> a beautiful necklace

   and _____ a ring with gold and diamonds.

ANALOGIES

An **analogy** compares two pairs of words. The relationship between the first pair of words is the same as the relationship between the second pair of words. Use the words in the box to complete the following analogies.

richness	technology	painstaking
injected	conservation	compressor

1. <u>Ancient</u> is to <u>crudeness</u> as <u>modern</u> is to _____.

2. <u>Tool</u> is to <u>hammer</u> as <u>machine</u> is to _____.

3. <u>Rough</u> is to <u>smooth</u> as <u>careless</u> is to _____.

4. <u>Nail</u> is to <u>hammered</u> as <u>needle</u> is to _____.

5. <u>Paleness</u> is to <u>dullness</u> as <u>deepness</u> is to _____.

6. <u>Destruction</u> is to <u>ruin</u> as <u>protection</u> is to _____.

Directions: Mark the space for the letter of the word that best completes the sentence.

Tip If you are not sure which word completes the sentence, do the best you can. Try to choose the answer that makes the most sense.

1. **Utensils** are kinds of _____.
   Ⓐ schedules   Ⓒ tools
   Ⓑ compressors   Ⓓ dishes

2. **Conservation** is the act of protecting or _____.
   Ⓕ communicating   Ⓗ wasting
   Ⓖ preserving   Ⓙ playing

3. Doing **painstaking** work is doing _____ work.
   Ⓐ digging   Ⓒ ingenious
   Ⓑ fast   Ⓓ careful

4. When a liquid is **injected**, it may be forced through a _____.
   Ⓕ needle   Ⓗ compressor
   Ⓖ pencil   Ⓙ television

5. Scientific **breakthroughs** are _____.
   Ⓐ secrets   Ⓒ discoveries
   Ⓑ utensils   Ⓓ weaknesses

6. **Richness** can mean _____.
   Ⓕ technology   Ⓗ painstaking
   Ⓖ paleness   Ⓙ deepness

7. New **technology** has to do with new _____.
   Ⓐ stories   Ⓒ colors
   Ⓑ methods   Ⓓ songs

8. If you **construct** a piece of jewelry, you _____ it.
   Ⓕ make   Ⓗ destroy
   Ⓖ inject   Ⓙ cook

9. An **ingenious** idea is a _____ one.
   Ⓐ stupid   Ⓒ easy
   Ⓑ painstaking   Ⓓ clever

10. A **compressor** is a kind of _____.
    Ⓕ richness   Ⓗ game
    Ⓖ machine   Ⓙ conservation

Review

1. If food is **abundant**, it is _____.
   Ⓐ plentiful   Ⓒ cooked
   Ⓑ happy   Ⓓ fertile

2. Someone who has **expectations** has _____.
   Ⓕ money   Ⓗ hopes
   Ⓖ homework   Ⓙ illness

3. A **category** is a kind of _____.
   Ⓐ chain   Ⓒ circle
   Ⓑ jewelry   Ⓓ group

4. A **concept** is a broad or general _____.
   Ⓕ current   Ⓗ island
   Ⓖ idea   Ⓙ beach

Writing

Gold is a very useful metal. Other metals have many uses, too. Think about some other metals, such as silver, copper, and aluminum. How are these metals used?

Write a paragraph telling about another metal and some of its uses. The pictures may give you some ideas. Use some vocabulary words in your writing.

Turn to "My Personal Word List" on page 132. Write some words from the story or other words that you would like to know more about. Use a dictionary to find the meanings.

MATHEMATICS
GLITTERING GOLD
LESSON 20

★ Read the story below. Think about the meanings of the **boldfaced** words. ★

America's Treasure House

Thirty-five miles south of Louisville, Kentucky, lies America's true house of treasure — Fort Knox. Since 1936, this army fort has been the home of the United States Gold Depository. The **subterranean** safe lies deep underneath the ground and is made of granite, steel, and concrete. It has the largest **capacity** in the world for storing gold.

At one time half the world's gold lay here in neat, **compact** stacks of bars, totalling almost $20 billion. Today the total gold **accumulated** in Fort Knox is worth much less. We don't know the dollar value, for that information is classified.

Each gold bar is 3 5/8 inches wide, 1 3/4 inches high, 7 inches long, and weighs 27 1/2 pounds. However, it is hard to **calculate** the gold's value since the price changes constantly.

The making of the gold bars is an involved process. At a special factory, hot, liquid gold is **purified** of any dirt or other elements, then poured into molds. Each gold bar is about 99.99 percent pure gold. It takes 1,000 **metric** tons, or two million pounds, of natural rock containing gold to make just one gold bar.

Few thieves would be foolish enough to try to break into Fort Knox's **vault**. The 40-foot-by-60-foot safe is covered on all sides by 25 inches of steel and concrete. The vault door alone weighs more than 20 tons and cannot be opened by one person. Combination locks open the vault door and several government workers know only one combination each. No one person can open all the locks.

Gold is not the only valuable that has been stored in Fort Knox's **treasury**. During World War II, some of our most priceless documents were placed there to **guarantee** their safety. They include the Declaration of Independence and the Constitution. Fort Knox is truly America's treasure house.

★ Go back to the story. Underline the words or sentences that give you a clue to the meaning of each **boldfaced** word. ★

CONTEXT CLUES

In each sentence, one word is underlined. That word sounds silly in the sentence. Choose the word from the box that should replace the silly word. Write it on the line.

capacity	subterranean	calculate	purified
accumulated	guarantee	vault	compact
treasury	metric		

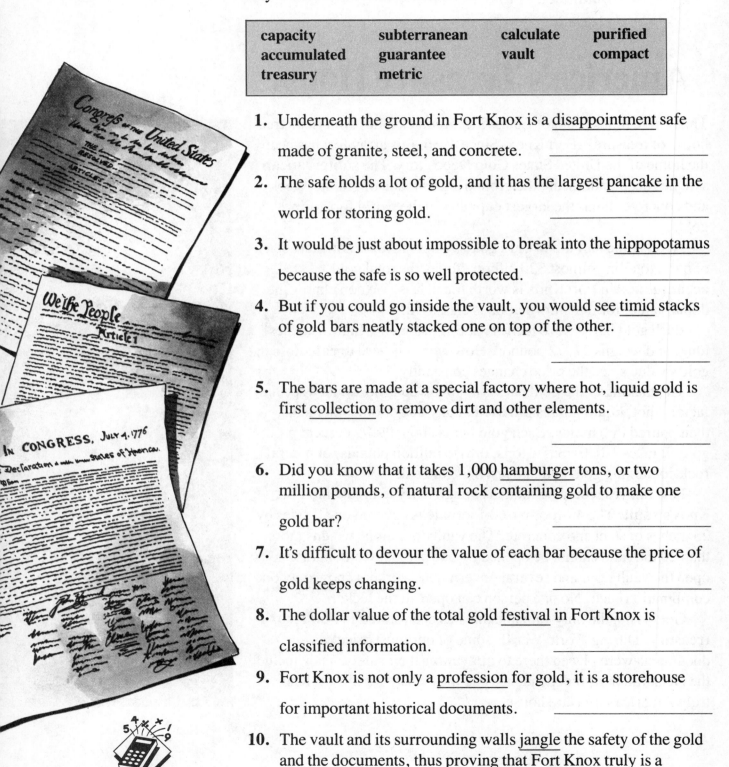

1. Underneath the ground in Fort Knox is a <u>disappointment</u> safe made of granite, steel, and concrete. _____

2. The safe holds a lot of gold, and it has the largest <u>pancake</u> in the world for storing gold. _____

3. It would be just about impossible to break into the <u>hippopotamus</u> because the safe is so well protected. _____

4. But if you could go inside the vault, you would see <u>timid</u> stacks of gold bars neatly stacked one on top of the other.

   _____

5. The bars are made at a special factory where hot, liquid gold is first <u>collection</u> to remove dirt and other elements.

   _____

6. Did you know that it takes 1,000 <u>hamburger</u> tons, or two million pounds, of natural rock containing gold to make one gold bar? _____

7. It's difficult to <u>devour</u> the value of each bar because the price of gold keeps changing. _____

8. The dollar value of the total gold <u>festival</u> in Fort Knox is classified information. _____

9. Fort Knox is not only a <u>profession</u> for gold, it is a storehouse for important historical documents. _____

10. The vault and its surrounding walls <u>jangle</u> the safety of the gold and the documents, thus proving that Fort Knox truly is a treasure house. _____

MULTIPLE MEANINGS

The words in the box have more than one meaning. Look for clues in each sentence to tell which meaning is being used. Write the letter of the meaning next to the correct sentence.

calculate
a. figure by using mathematics
b. plan beforehand; estimate

subterranean
a. below ground
b. done out of sight, secretly; hidden

vault
a. a strongly protected place for keeping valuables
b. to leap or jump over

compact
a. closely and tightly packed together
b. a small case for carrying face powder

_____ **1.** We can calculate our chances of winning the election.

_____ **2.** She will calculate the problem using multiplication.

_____ **3.** We put our valuables in a subterranean vault.

_____ **4.** It became clear that there was a subterranean plot.

_____ **5.** I was able to vault over a bar that was five feet high.

_____ **6.** You should keep important documents in a vault.

_____ **7.** I dropped the compact and the powder spilled all over.

_____ **8.** The sardines are compact in these cans.

WORD SENSE

Read each phrase. Check the Dictionary to see if the words make sense together. If they do, write yes on the line. If they do not, write a new word that does make sense with the underlined word.

1. metric wings _____

2. treasury glass _____

3. accumulated wealth _____

4. purified the table _____

5. uncle capacity _____

6. guarantee safety _____

WORD MAP

Use the vocabulary words in the box to complete the word map about Fort Knox. Add other words that you know to each group.

compact	treasury	subterranean	capacity
vault	purified		

What It Is

1. _____ house

2. _____

3. _____

4. _____

What It Contains

1. _____ place

2. solid _____

3. large _____

4. _____

FORT KNOX

Words That Describe the Gold

1. _____

2. _____

3. _____

4. _____

Directions: Read the phrase. Look for the word or words that have the same or almost the same meaning as the boldfaced word. Mark the answer space for your choice.

 Think about the meaning of the boldfaced word before you choose an answer. Don't be fooled by a word that looks similar to the boldfaced word.

1. **subterranean** safe
   Ⓐ cardboard
   Ⓑ underground
   Ⓒ compact
   Ⓓ stubborn

2. **calculate** the time
   Ⓕ figure out
   Ⓖ quote wrongly
   Ⓗ collect
   Ⓙ introduce

3. largest **capacity**
   Ⓐ cranberry
   Ⓑ weight
   Ⓒ available space
   Ⓓ crowd

4. **purified** the gold
   Ⓕ pursued
   Ⓖ cleaned
   Ⓗ accumulated
   Ⓙ injected

5. **metric** ton
   Ⓐ a weight
   Ⓑ a height
   Ⓒ a vault
   Ⓓ gold

6. total **accumulated**
   Ⓕ purified
   Ⓖ stolen
   Ⓗ collected
   Ⓙ accompanied

7. **compact** stacks
   Ⓐ tightly packed
   Ⓑ loosely folded
   Ⓒ subterranean
   Ⓓ powdered

8. steel **vault**
   Ⓕ pole
   Ⓖ tool
   Ⓗ door
   Ⓙ safe

9. Fort Knox's **treasury**
   Ⓐ terrace
   Ⓑ storehouse
   Ⓒ war
   Ⓓ combination

10. **guarantee** safety
   Ⓕ avoid
   Ⓖ admire
   Ⓗ refuse
   Ⓙ promise

Review

1. **defensive** measures
   Ⓐ dense
   Ⓑ dangerous
   Ⓒ protective
   Ⓓ awesome

2. **solitary** life
   Ⓕ crowded
   Ⓖ lonely
   Ⓗ boring
   Ⓙ solid

3. **renowned** person
   Ⓐ famous
   Ⓑ fat
   Ⓒ brilliant
   Ⓓ unknown

4. ropes **elevated**
   Ⓕ buried
   Ⓖ stretched
   Ⓗ entered
   Ⓙ lifted

5. **ingenious** machine
   Ⓐ interesting
   Ⓑ long-lasting
   Ⓒ clever
   Ⓓ dangerous

Writing

Both gold and historical documents were put in Fort Knox for safekeeping. What objects, documents, or letters do you have that you would place in a safe for protection? What makes these things valuable to you?

Write a paragraph telling about these things. Use some vocabulary words in your writing.

_____

_____

_____

_____

_____

_____

_____

_____

_____

_____

_____

_____

_____

_____

_____

_____

_____

_____

_____

Turn to "My Personal Word List" on page 132. Write some words from the story or other words that you would like to know more about. Use a dictionary to find the meanings.

★ To review the words in Lessons 17–20, turn to page 129. ★

REVIEW

Read each clue. Then write the word from the box that fits the clue. Use the Dictionary if you need help.

lifeline	plateau	wielding	receded
fertile	desolate	ordeal	slush
remote	evaporated		

1. If you are able to grow many crops on a piece of land, the land could be described as this. _____

2. If a country can only be reached by boat, it could be called this. _____

3. At this kind of place, you would be standing on flat ground high in the air. _____

4. When the flood waters began to pull back, they did this.

   _____

5. When you walk through melting snow, you move through this. _____

6. You can use this word to tell what happened to morning dew when the sun hit it. _____

7. A desert or ghost town could be described as this.

   _____

8. If you have survived an accident, you have experienced this. _____

9. This piece of equipment would come in handy if someone fell out of a boat. _____

10. This word tells what a good lumberjack is doing when he cuts down trees with his axe.

   _____

REVIEW

Read each question. Think about the meaning of the underlined word. Then use <u>yes</u> or <u>no</u> to answer the question. Use the Dictionary if you need help.

1. If you are lost and need to find the way home, would an <u>illusion</u> come in handy? _____

2. If you do not understand how to play a new video game, will a <u>demonstration</u> of it probably help? _____

3. Is World War II a <u>significant</u> event in world history? _____

4. Could a speaker use an example to <u>illustrate</u> a point in his speech? _____

5. If you <u>established</u> a soccer club, did you make sure no one joined it? _____

6. Is a hamster <u>illiterate</u>? _____

7. Do identical twins look <u>distinctly</u> different? _____

8. Would most people be likely to <u>ponder</u> a big decision? _____

9. Is an elephant highly <u>portable</u>? _____

10. Does your shoe <u>monitor</u> your foot? _____

11. Would most students enjoy having a large <u>quantity</u> of homework? _____

12. Is taking a bath an <u>alternative</u> to taking a shower? _____

REVIEW

Read each question. Think about the meaning of the underlined word. Then use <u>yes</u> or <u>no</u> to answer the question. Use the Dictionary if you need help.

1. Is sharpening your pencil <u>strenuous</u> work? _____

2. If you cannot see very well, should you think about buying some <u>spectators</u>? _____

3. Would you expect to see <u>pomp</u> at a royal wedding? _____

4. If your favorite singer were coming to perform at your school, would your feelings be <u>fervent</u>? _____

5. If you need to know where you left your shoes, should you <u>gauge</u> them? _____

6. Would you find a <u>discus</u> growing in the desert? _____

7. Would you expect a squirrel to be <u>hoarding</u> nuts in the fall? _____

8. Could an athlete's <u>attitude</u> affect the way she competes? _____

9. Would you expect to find a <u>stadium</u> full of fish? _____

10. Would a race car driver be <u>reluctant</u> to drive fast in a race? _____

11. If you need to slice apples for a pie, do you need to <u>sacrifice</u> them? _____

12. If you are a <u>capable</u> worker, can you get the job done? _____

REVIEW

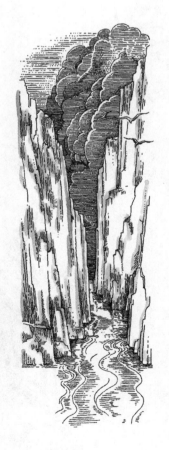

Read each clue. Then write the word from the box that fits the clue. Use the Dictionary if you need help.

terrains	temporary	souvenir	majestic
beheld	withstood	nomads	tedious
mummy	assisted		

1. During a thunderstorm, a blackout is usually this.

   _____

2. When you ride a bicycle over mountains and through valleys, you travel across these. _____

3. If a bridge did not fall during an earthquake, we say it did this. _____

4. A huge snowcapped mountain could be described with this word. _____

5. If you went to a museum and saw a painting, you did this to the painting. _____

6. Counting all the grains of sand on a beach could be called this kind of task. _____

7. If you went to Egypt and looked inside a tomb, you might see this. _____

8. If you bought a T-shirt at Disney World to remember your vacation, you bought this. _____

9. You would not find these people at the same address all their lives. _____

10. If you helped your mother plant a garden, you did this.

    _____

REVIEW

Read each clue. Then write the word from the box that fits the clue. Use the Dictionary if you need help.

distrusted	abundant	epidemic	expectations
persisted	vault	ingenious	subterranean
dynamite	construct		

1. When you build model airplanes, you do this to them.

    _____

2. If thousands of people in a city get the flu at the same time, the city has this. _____

3. If you think of something new and clever, you might be described as this. _____

4. A story that has been retold year after year has done this.

    _____

5. You can use this word to describe caves that are found under the ground. _____

6. If you hope to receive certain gifts on your birthday, you have these. _____

7. This substance is designed to cause an explosion.

    _____

8. If you are planning to throw a big party, your food supply should be this. _____

9. If you need a safe place to keep jewelry, you can use this.

    _____

10. If you didn't trust someone, this is what you did.

    _____

REVIEW AND WRITE

In this book you have read about many special places, from natural wonders such as the Nile River and the White Cliffs of Dover to human-made wonders such as Mt. Rushmore.

Pretend you are a reporter assigned to write about a new world wonder. Describe what makes this new place so amazing. Is it a natural wonder, or one that has been built by people? Tell what effect it will have on our world. Use some vocabulary words you have learned.

_____
_____
_____
_____
_____
_____
_____
_____
_____
_____
_____
_____
_____
_____
_____
_____
_____
_____
_____

MY PERSONAL WORD LIST

This is your word list. Here you can write words from the stories. You can also write other words that you would like to know more about. Use a dictionary to find the meaning of each word. Then write the meaning next to the word.

UNIT 1
RAMBLING RIVERS

UNIT 2
EXTRAORDINARY
INVENTIONS

My Personal Word List

UNIT 3
THE OLYMPIC DREAM

UNIT 4
WORLD WONDERS

UNIT 5
GLITTERING GOLD

DICTIONARY

ENTRY

Each word in a dictionary is called an **entry word**. Study the parts of an entry in the sample shown below. Think about how each part will help you when you read and write.

① **Entry Word** An entry word is boldfaced. A dot is used to divide the word into syllables.

② **Pronunciation** This special spelling shows you how to say the word. Look at the pronunciation key below. It tells you the symbols that stand for sounds.

③ **Part of Speech** The abbreviation tells you the part of speech. In this entry *v.* stands for verb.

④ **Words with Spelling Changes** When the spelling of a word changes after *-ed* or *-ing* is added, the spelling is shown in an entry.

⑤ **Definition** A definition is given for each entry word. The definition tells what the word means.

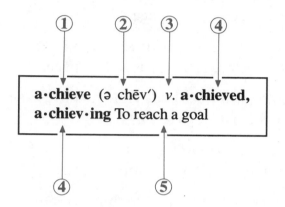

a·chieve (ə chēv′) *v.* a·chieved, a·chiev·ing To reach a goal

PRONUNCIATION KEY

A **pronunciation key** is a helpful tool. It shows you the symbols, or special signs, for the sounds in English. Next to each symbol is a sample word for that sound. Use the key to help you with the pronunciation given after each entry word.

a	at, bad	d	dear, soda, bad
ā	ape, pain, day, break	f	five, defend, leaf, off, cough, elephant
ä	father, car, heart	g	game, ago, fog, egg
âr	care, pair, bear, their, where	h	hat, ahead
e	end, pet, said, heaven, friend	hw	white, whether, which
ē	equal, me, feet, team, piece, key	j	joke, enjoy, gem, page, edge
i	it, big, English, hymn	k	kite, bakery, seek, tack, cat
ī	ice, fine, lie, my	l	lid, sailor, feel, ball, allow
îr	ear, deer, here, pierce	m	man, family, dream
o	odd, hot, watch	n	not, final, pan, knife
ō	old, oat, toe, low	ng	long, singer, pink
ô	coffee, all, taught, law, fought	p	pail, repair, soap, happy
ôr	order, fork, horse, story, pour	r	ride, parent, wear, more, marry
oi	oil, toy	s	sit, aside, pets, cent, pass
ou	out, now	sh	shoe, washer, fish, mission, nation
u	up, mud, love, double	t	tag, pretend, fat, button, dressed
ū	use, mule, cue, feud, few	th	thin, panther, both
ü	rule, true, food	th	this, mother, smooth
u̇	put, wood, should	v	very, favor, wave
ûr	burn, hurry, term, bird, word, courage	w	wet, weather, reward
ə	about, taken, pencil, lemon, circus	y	yes, onion
b	bat, above, job	z	zoo, lazy, jazz, rose, dogs, houses
ch	chin, such, match	zh	vision, treasure, seizure

DICTIONARY

A

a·bun·dant (ə bun′dənt) *adj.* Plentiful. page 108

ac·cess (ak′ses) *n.* The chance or right to approach or use. page 47

ac·cu·mu·lat·ed (ə kū′myə lā tid) *adj.* Collected; gathered together. page 119

ag·ile (aj′əl, aj′īl) *adj.* Able to move easily and quickly. page 71

ag·ri·cul·tur·al (ag′ri kul′chər əl) *adj.* Having to do with farming. page 6

al·ter·na·tive (ôl tûr′nə tiv) *n.* Another possibility. page 47

an·tic·i·pa·tion (an tis′ə pā′shən) *n.* Hope; looking forward to or expecting something. page 102

ar·chae·ol·o·gy (är′kē ol′ə jē) *n.* The science that studies objects from the past. page 90

ar·chi·tec·tur·al (är′ki tek′chər əl) *adj.* Having to do with designing and erecting buildings. They looked at the architectural plans for a large house. page 95

ar·chives (är′kīvz) *n.* Records. page 66

as·sist (ə sist′) *v.* To help. page 78

at·tain (ə tān′) *v.* To gain through effort. page 66

at·ten·dance (ə ten′dəns) *n.* The number of people who come to an event. page 54

at·ti·tude (at′i tüd′, at′i tūd′) *n.* State of mind; way of thinking. Jan's cheerful attitude makes her fun to be around. page 71

au·to·mat·i·cal·ly (ô′tə mat′ik lē) *adv.* Done without outside help. page 47

awe·some (ô′səm) *adj.* Causing wonder and amazement. page 95

B

back·pack·ing (bak′pak′ing) *adj.* Hiking using a pack to carry supplies. page 23

be·held (bi held′) *v. past tense of* **behold** Looked at; saw. page 78

ben·e·fit (ben′ə fit) *v.* To receive good from. page 30

bi·fo·cal (bī fō′kəl) *adj.* Having glass lenses that allow one to see both close-up and at a distance. page 30

break·through (brāk′thrü) *n.* An important discovery that helps solve a problem. page 114

brink (bringk) *n.* Edge of a steep place. page 18

bur·i·al (ber′ē əl) *n.* The placing of a dead body in a grave. page 90

bust (bust) *n.* Sculpture of a person's head and shoulders. page 78

C

cal•cu•late (kal′kyə lāt′) *v.* **cal•cu•lat•ed,**
cal•cu•lat•ing To figure out using
arithmetic. page 119

can•di•date (kan′di dāt′) *n.* One who
seeks an office or honor. page 66

ca•pa•bil•i•ty (kā′pə bil′i tē) *n.*
ca•pa•bil•i•ties The ability to do work.
page 47

ca•pa•ble (kā′pə bəl) *adj.* Able. page 66

ca•pac•i•ty (kə pas′i tē) *n.* **ca•pac•i•ties**
Size; the ability to hold or contain. A
bottle that has this capacity can hold five
gallons of liquid. page 119

car•ti•lage (kär′tə lij) *n.* The body tissue
that connects bones. Don could not walk
because he had torn the cartilage in his
knee. page 60

carv•ing (kär′ving) *n.* A piece of art made
by cutting stone or wood. page 78

cas•cade (kas kād′) *v.* **cas•ca•ded,**
cas•cad•ing To tumble down from a
higher to a lower place. page 23

cat•e•go•ry (kat′i gôr′ē) *n.* **cat•e•go•ries**
Class; kind. *Jack and the Beanstalk*
belongs to the category of fairy tales.
page 109

chasm (kaz′əm) *n.* A deep canyon or
crack. page 18

cleft (kleft) *n.* An opening or crack.
page 18

clum•si•ly (klum′zə lē) *adv.* In an
awkward way. page 60

com•pact (kəm pakt′, kom′pakt) *adj.*
Packed closely together in a small space.
Pierre folded his tent and sleeping bag
into a light, compact bundle. page 119

com•pet•i•tive (kəm pet′i tiv) *adj.* Driven
by the desire to succeed or win. page 54

com•pre•hend (kom′pri hend′) *v.* To
understand. page 30

com•pres•sor (kəm pres′ər) *n.* A machine
that squeezes a liquid or gas. page 114

con•cept (kon′sept) *n.* Idea; mental
picture. Americans believe in the
concept that everyone is created equal.
page 109

con•quer•or (kong′kər ər) *n.* One who
overcomes another by force. page 108

con•quest (kon′kwest, kong′kwest) *n.*
The act of taking over by force. page 95

con•ser•va•tion (kon′ser vā′shən) *n.* The
concern for and protection of natural
resources, such as land. page 114

con•struct (kən strukt′) *v.* To make.
page 114

con•tempt (kən tempt′) *n.* Scorn; lack of
respect. page 37

con•test•ant (kən tes′tənt) *n.* A person
who takes part in a contest. page 54

con•trast (kon′trast) *n.* A great difference
between things. The colors of leaves in
fall show great contrast with their colors
in summer. page 42

craze (krāz) *n.* Madness; an enthusiasm
shared by many people. page 102

cross-coun•try (krôs′kun′trē) *adj.* Moving across open country. page 66

D

ded•i•ca•tion (ded′i kā′shən) *n.* The willingness to devote great effort to a special purpose. page 71

de•fen•sive (di fen′siv) *adj.* Used for protection. page 95

del•ta (del′tə) *n.* A three-sided piece of land deposited at the end of a river. The delta of the Nile was formed out of sand that fell from its slow-moving waters. page 6

dem•on•stra•tion (dem′ən strā′shən) *n.* Display, often intended to prove an idea or theory. page 37

de•par•ture (di pär′chər) *n.* Starting out; leaving. page 23

des•o•late (des′ə lit) *adj.* Deserted; without inhabitants. page 18

de•vise (di vīz′) *v.* **de•vised, de•vis•ing** To invent; think up. page 42

di•ag•o•nal (dī ag′ə nəl) *adj.* Slanted; going up and down at an angle. page 90

dis•cus (dis′kəs) *adj.* Having to do with sporting contests in which a heavy disc is thrown. page 60

dis•tinct•ly (di stingk′lē) *adv.* Without question; definitely. page 42

dis•trust (dis trust′) *v.* To have no trust in; be suspicious of. page 102

dra•mat•ic (drə mat′ik) *adj.* Exciting; theatrical. page 78

dy•na•mite (dī′nə mīt′) *n.* A mixture that blows up with great force; an explosive. page 102

E

ear•phones (îr′fōnz′) *n.* Listening devices worn over the ears. page 42

ec•o•nom•ic (ek′ə nom′ik, ē′kə nom′ik) *adj.* Having to do with money. The discovery of oil changed the economic state of the poor country. page 108

e•lec•tri•cal (i lek′tri kəl) *adj.* Having to do with electricity. page 42

e•lec•tron (i lek′tron) *adj.* Made up of the very small particles that carry electricity. The electron gun in a TV shoots tiny particles that light up the screen. page 42

e•lec•tron•ic (i lek tron′ik) *adj.* Working by electricity. page 47

el•e•vate (el′ə vāt′) *v.* **el•e•vat•ed, el•e•vat•ing** To raise; lift. page 90

em•bed•ded (em bed′id) *adj.* Buried; set in. The explorers found dinosaur bones embedded in the rocks of the cliff. page 18

e•merge (i mûrj′) *v.* **e•merged, e•merg•ing** To come out. page 84

emp•ty-hand•ed (emp′tē han′did) *adj.* With nothing to show for one's efforts. page 102

en•thu•si•as•tic (en thü′zē as′tik) *adj.* Interested and excited. page 71

ep·i·dem·ic (ep´i dem´ik) *n.* A sickness that spreads quickly. page 102

e·qua·tor (i kwā´tər) *n.* An imaginary line around the middle of the earth. page 6

e·ro·sion (i rō´zhen) *n.* The slow wearing away of rock by wind, rain, and sand. Erosion slowly turned the great mountain into low, gentle hills. page 18

es·tab·lish (e stab´lish) *v.* To start; set up. page 30

e·vap·o·rate (i vap´ə rāt´) *v.* **e·vap·o·rat·ed, e·vap·o·rat·ing** To change from a liquid to a gas. page 6

ex·pec·ta·tion (ek´spek tā´shən) *n.* The act of looking forward to something you think will probably happen. page 109

ex·ten·sion (ek sten´shən) *n.* Something added on. The extension to the house gave the family two new rooms. page 95

F

fa·cil·i·ty (fə sil´i tē) *n.* **fa·cil·i·ties** Buildings and equipment that serve a special purpose. page 60

fac·tor (fak´tər) *n.* Something that helps bring about a result. A factor in Valerie's success at school is her love of learning. page 66

fa·tigued (fə tēgd´) *adj.* Tired. page 71

fer·tile (fûr´təl) *adj.* Well suited to plant growth. page 6

fer·vent (fûr´vənt) *adj.* Having or showing deep and warm feeling. page 71

found·er (foun´dər) *n.* The person who starts something. page 30

froth·ing (frôth´ing) *adj.* Producing foam. page 13

fun·da·men·tal (fun´də men´təl) *adj.* Basic. The curve is a fundamental pitch in baseball. page 71

fu·til·i·ty (fū til´i tē) *n.* **fu·til·i·ties** Uselessness. page 37

G

gauge (gāj) *v.* To measure carefully; determine the amount or distance. page 66

gild·ed (gild´id) *adj.* Covered with gold. The gilded statue gleamed golden-yellow. page 108

guar·an·tee (gar´ən tē´) *v.* **guar·an·teed** To make certain or secure. page 119

H

hem·or·rhage (hem´ər ij, hem´rij) *v.* To bleed a great deal. page 61

hoarding (hôrd) *adj.* Carefully saving for future use. page 61

home·sick·ness (hōm´sik´nis) *n.* A deep longing for home. page 102

home·stead (hōm´sted´) *n.* A house, other buildings, and the land around it. page 102

host (hōst) *n.* A large number. page 60

husk•y (hus´kē) *adj.* **husk•i•er, husk•i•est** Big and strong. page 60

I

il•lit•er•ate (i lit´ər it) *adj.* Unable to read or write. page 36

il•lu•sion (i lü´zhen) *n.* Something that seems to be real but is not. Movies create the <u>illusion</u> of motion by quickly showing many still pictures. page 42

il•lus•trate (il´ə strāt´, i lus´trāt´) *v.* **il•lus•trat•ed, il•lus•trat•ing** To make clear; prove. page 30

in•cline (in´klīn´) *n.* Slope; slanted surface. It was not easy to walk up the steep <u>incline</u> of the ramp. page 90

in•dus•try (in´də strē) *n.* **in•dus•tries** The making of goods to be sold. page 6

in•field (in´fēld´) *n.* The inner part of a playing field. page 60

in•gen•ious (in jēn´yəs) *adj.* Clever and unexpected. page 114

in•ject (in jekt´) *v.* To put a liquid inside, as with a needle. page 114

in•scrip•tion (in skrip´shən) *n.* Words carved or written on something. page 78

in•te•ri•or (in tîr´ē ər) *n.* The inside. page 18

i•so•lat•ed (ī´sə lāt´id) *adj.* Separated or set apart from a group. page 108

J

jave•lin (jav´lin) *n.* A spear thrown in sporting contests. page 54

L

la•bor•er (lā´bər ər) *n.* Worker. page 95

leg•end•ar•y (lej´ən der´ē) *adj.* Larger-than-life; fabled. The <u>legendary</u> knights of the Round Table performed many brave deeds in the days of King Arthur. page 36

lei•sure (lē´zhər, lezh´ər) *n.* Free time. page 36

life•line (līf´līn´) *n.* A rope thrown to save a person in the water. page 23

lim•it•less (lim´it lis) *adj.* Without any end. page 47

loom (lüm) *v.* To appear large and threatening. The big old house seemed to <u>loom</u> over them in the fog. page 84

lurch (lûrch) *n.* A sudden rolling or swaying movement. page 13

M

ma•jes•tic (mə jes´tik) *adj.* Impressive; grand or noble-looking. page 78

ma•nip•u•late (mə nip´yə lāt´) *v.* **ma•nip•u•lat•ed, ma•nip•u•lat•ing** To control or work with the hands. page 47

met•ric (met´rik) *adj.* As measured in the metric system. A <u>metric</u> ton is 204 pounds heavier than an ordinary ton. page 119

mid•stream (mid´strēm´) *adv.* In the middle of a stream or river. page 23

min•i•a•ture (min´ē ə chər, min´ə chər) *adj.* Very small. page 42

mon•i•tor (mon´i tər) *v.* To check; keep watch over. They used a TV camera to <u>monitor</u> people who came into the building at night. page 47

more•o•ver (môr ō´ver) *adv.* Also; besides. page 37

mum•my (mum´ē) *n.* **mum•mies** A body that is preserved after death. page 90

N

no•mad (nō´mad) *n.* A person who belongs to a group of people who have no permanent home, but move from place to place. page 95

nook (nůk) *n.* A small, out-of-the-way place. page 85

O

or•deal (ôr dēl´, ôr´dēl) *n.* An experience that is painful or difficult. page 23

P

pains•tak•ing (pānz´tā´king) *adj.* Very careful. page 114

pat•ent (pat´ənt) *v.* To obtain government protection for an invention. page 30

per•sist (pər sist´) *v.* To last for some time; continue. page 109

phar•aoh (fâr´ō) *n.* A king of ancient Egypt. page 90

piv•ot (piv´ət) *v.* To turn. page 23

pla•teau (pla tō´) *n.* A high, flat piece of land. page 18

pomp (pomp) *n.* Splendid or showy display. page 54

pon•der (pon´dər) *v.* To think about. Her cat's tricks made Janice <u>ponder</u> the question of animal intelligence. page 36

port•a•ble (pôr´tə bəl) *adj.* Easily carried. page 42

pre•dic•a•ment (pri dik´ə mənt) *n.* Problem; bad or difficult situation. page 84

pre•dic•tion (pri dik´shən) *n.* Something a person claims will happen in the future. page 30

pre•vail•ing (pri vā´ling) *adj.* The greatest in strength; the most common. In winter the <u>prevailing</u> winds blow from the north. page 84

pro•claim (prə klām´) *v.* To declare publicly. page 54

pro•gres•sive (prə gres´iv) *adj.* New and different. page 30

pro•trude (prō trüd´) *v.* **pro•trud•ed, pro•trud•ing** To stick out. page 18

pu•ri•fy (pyůr´ə fī´) *v.* **pu•ri•fied** To rid of unwanted things; make pure. page 119

Q

quan•ti•ty (kwon´ti tē) *n.* **quan•ti•ties**
Amount. page 47

R

rap•ids (rap´idz) *n.* Fast-moving waters in a river. page 13

re•cede (ri sēd´) *v.* **re•ced•ed**, **re•ced•ing** To pull back or withdraw. page 18

re•luc•tant (ri luk´tənt) *adj.* Unwilling. page 61

re•mote (ri mōt´) *adj.* **re•mot•er**, **re•mot•est** Far away; difficult to reach. page 23

re•nowned (ri nound´) *adj.* Very famous. page 78

res•er•voir (rez´ər vwär´) *n.* The lake created by a dam; a place where water is stored. page 6

res•o•lute•ly (rez´ə lüt´lē) *adv.* In a firm and determined way. Robert and Marguerite set out resolutely to climb the mountain. page 13

re•source (rē´sôrs´, ri sôrs´, rē´zôrs´, ri zôrs´) *n.* A supply of something that can be used to produce useful or valuable things. One great resource of the country is its rich soil. page 6

re•tort (ri tôrt´) *v.* To answer; reply sharply. page 13

rich•ness (rich´nis) *n.* The state of being vivid or intense. page 114

rid•i•cule (rid´i kūl´) *n.* Something said to make fun of another person. page 37

S

sac•ri•fice (sak´rə fīs´) *v.* **sac•ri•ficed**, **sac•ri•fic•ing** To give up for the sake of something else. page 71

score•board (skôr´bôrd´) *n.* A large board that shows scores and times in athletic contests. page 66

sculp•tor (skulp´tər) *n.* An artist who creates figures from stone, wood, or clay. page 78

ses•sion (sesh´ən) *n.* A single period of time. At each session, the young magicians learned a new trick. page 71

shan•ty (shan´tē) *n.* **shan•ties** A roughly built, run-down shack. page 102

shore•line (shôr´līn´) *n.* The place where shore and water meet. page 23

sig•nif•i•cant (sig nif´i kənt) *adj.* Important. Edison's significant inventions include the electric light and phonograph. page 30

silt (silt) *n.* Fine, rich soil carried in moving water. page 6

slosh (slosh) *v.* To move through water, making splashing sounds. page 13

slush (slush) *n.* Partially melted snow. page 13

sol•i•tar•y (sol´i ter´ē) *adj.* Without other people. page 102

sou•ve•nir (sü´və nir´, sü´və nîr´) *n.* A reminder of a place or an event. page 85

spec•ta•tor (spek´tā tər) *n.* A person who watches something; viewer. page 66

spir•i•tu•al (spir´i chü əl) *adj.* Religious; sacred. page 90

spon•sor (spon´sər) *v.* To pay for; support. Governments often <u>sponsor</u> science research. page 109

sta•di•um (stā´dē əm) *n.* An enclosed roofless area used for sporting and other events. page 54

star•board (stär´bərd) *adj.* On the right side of a ship when one is facing forward. page 85

stop•watch (stop´woch´) *n.* A watch used to time speeds in contests. page 66

stor•age (stôr´ij) *adj.* Having space to save something for later use. All student records are kept in the school computer's <u>storage</u> area. page 47

stren•u•ous (stren´ū əs) *adj.* Requiring great effort. page 54

sub•ter•ra•ne•an (sub´tə rā´nē ən) *adj.* Underground. page 119

sum•mit (sum´it) *n.* The highest part; top. page 78

su•preme (sə prēm´) *adj.* Highest; most important. page 54

sym•pa•thy (sim´pə thē) *n.* **sym•pa•thies** The sharing and understanding of another person's feelings. page 36

T

tech•nol•o•gy (tek nol´ə jē) *n.* Advanced tools and machinery. Space rockets could not be built without today's <u>technology</u>. page 114

te•di•ous (tē´dē əs, tē´jəs) *adj.* Slow and boring. page 90

tem•pest (tem´pist) *n.* A violent storm; furious commotion. page 23

tem•po•rar•y (tem´pə rer´ē) *adj.* Not long-lasting; short-lived. page 85

ter•rain (tə rān´, te rān´) *n.* A certain area of land. page 95

there•af•ter (thâr af´tər) *adv.* After that. page 85

treas•ur•y (trezh´ə rē) *n.* **treas•ur•ies** A place where valuable things are stored. page 119

tri•an•gu•lar (trī ang´gyə lər) *adj.* Having a three-sided shape. page 90

trib•ute (trib´ūt) *n.* Something done or given to show respect or to worship. The face on a penny is a <u>tribute</u> to one of our great presidents, Abraham Lincoln. page 54

U

un•furled (un fûrld´) *adj.* Unrolled; spread out. page 85

u•ni•ty (ū´ni tē) *n.* **u•ni•ties** The state of being a whole. page 95

u•ten•sil (ū ten´səl) *n.* A useful tool or container. A fork is a common utensil. page 114

V _____

vault (vôlt) *n.* A room or box for keeping valuables. page 119

vis•u•al (vizh´ü əl) *adj.* Having to do with things that are seen. page 42

vi•tal•i•ty (vī tal´i tē) *n.* Liveliness; energy. page 71

W _____

whirl•pool (hwûrl´pül´, wûrl´pül´) *n.* Water that is moving rapidly in a circle. page 13

wield•ing (wēld´ing) *adj.* Using skillfully. Wielding her hoe, Letty quickly weeded the garden. page 13

with•stood (with stůd´, with stůd´) *v. past tense of* **withstand** Resisted; survived. page 95

wor•ship (wûr´ship) *v.* **wor•shipped, wor•ship•ping** To pray to; show respect and honor for. page 6

wrench (rench) *v.* To twist sharply. page 13